W9-ANH-431

WASHINGTON SQUARE

STYLES OF MONEY

TWAYNE'S MASTERWORK STUDIES

Robert Lecker, General Editor

WASHINGTON SQUARE

Styles of Money

Ian F. A. Bell

TWAYNE PUBLISHERS • NEW YORK
Maxwell Macmillan Canada • *Toronto*
Maxwell Macmillan International • *New York Oxford Singapore Sydney*

Twayne's Masterwork Studies No. 116

Washington Square: Styles of Money
Ian F. A. Bell

Twayne Publishers   Maxwell Macmillan Canada, Inc.
Macmillan Publishing Company   1200 Eglinton Avenue East
866 Third Avenue   Suite 200
New York, New York 10022   Don Mills, Ontario M3C 3N1

Library of Congress Cataloging-in-Publication Data

Bell, Ian F. A.
    Washington Square : styles of money / by Ian F. A. Bell.
        p.   cm. — (Twayne's masterwork studies ; no. 116)
    Includes bibliographical references and index.
    ISBN 0-8057-8359-8 — ISBN 0-8057-8596-5
    1. James, Henry, 1843-1916. Washington Square. 2. Money in
literature.   I. Title.   II. Series.
    PS2116.W333   1993
    813'.4—dc20   92-42510
                                                                                      CIP

The paper used in this publication meets the minimum requirements of American
National Standard for Information Sciences—Permanence of Paper for Printed
Library Materials. ANSI Z3948-1984.∞™

10 9 8 7 6 5 4 3 2 1 (hc)
10 9 8 7 6 5 4 3 2 1 (pb)

Printed in the United States of America

For
Timothy Bell
and
Ben Bell

CONTENTS

NOTE ON THE REFERENCES
AND ACKNOWLEDGMENTS

Throughout, I have used the Penguin edition of *Washington Square* (1984). The bulk of my secondary sources have been taken from books rather than journal articles; the former are not only more accessible but, in general, contain the most useful discussions. A significant portion of the secondary sources are works of historical documentation. These are not to be considered merely as "background" to the novel but as bodies of material that are profoundly embedded within the novel's principal preoccupations.

I am grateful to Nicola Bradbury of the University of Reading and to my historian colleagues at Keele, Martin Crawford and Robert Garson, for their guidance during the book's gestation. Amanda Gautby translated the hieroglyphics of my script onto the word processor with a sharp eye. Cindy Buck, the Twayne copyeditor, not only tightened my prose, but suggested that Austin Sloper's name may well carry an echo of Jane Austen.

CHRONOLOGY: HENRY JAMES'S LIFE AND WORKS

1843	Born 15 April in Washington Place, New York City. Both of his parents (Henry James, Sr., and Mary Robertson Walsh) are powerful personalities, belonging to prosperous families whose American lineage began in the last quarter of the eighteenth century. His father, reacting against the Presbyterianism of his immediate background, avails himself of the more freethinking attitudes of his day, most notably through the works of the French social theorist Charles Fourier and the Swedish mystic Emanuel Swedenborg, and through acquaintance with the more radical of contemporary intellectuals, such as Margaret Fuller and Ralph Waldo Emerson. Henry James, Jr., is the second of five children, the most noteworthy of whom is his elder brother William (born 11 January 1842), the philosopher who will become well known for his association with the pragmatist school of thought.
1843–1855	Childhood spent in Albany and New York City, apart from a trip to England in 1844. Garth Wilkinson (Wilky) born 21 July 1845; Robertson (Rob) born 29 August 1846; Alice born 7 August 1848.
1855–1859	Educated at schools in Geneva, London, Paris, and Bonn. Family returns to the United States to live in Newport, Rhode Island. Forms friendships with Thomas Sergeant Perry and John La Farge.
1859–1860	Education continues in Geneva and Bonn.
1860–1862	Returns to Newport and begins close friendship with cousin Minnie Temple. Reads Balzac, Musset, Browning, and Hawthorne.
1862–1863	Enters Harvard Law School but soon withdraws to attempt a writing career.
1864	Family moves to Boston. Publishes first tale, "A Tragedy of Error" (unsigned), in *Continental Monthly* (February) and be-

gins reviewing for the *North American Review*, forming close friendships with its editor, Charles Eliot Norton, and his sister Grace.

1865	Publishes first signed tale, "The Story of a Year," in *Atlantic Monthly* (March) and begins reviewing for *The Nation*.
1866–1868	Family moves to Cambridge. Begins friendship with William Dean Howells.
1869–1870	Travels in England, France, and Italy. Meets Leslie Stephen, William Morris, Dante Gabriel Rossetti, Edward Burne-Jones, John Ruskin, Charles Darwin, and George Eliot. Minnie Temple dies.
1870	Returns to Cambridge in May.
1871	Publishes first novel, *Watch and Ward*.
1872–1874	Travels in England, France, Switzerland, Italy, Austria, and Germany. Writes travel sketches for *The Nation*, establishes friendships with James Russell Lowell, Fanny Kemble, and William Wetmore Story, and meets Matthew Arnold.
1874	Returns to America in September.
1875	Now beginning to support himself from writing. Tries, unsuccessfully, to live in New York and publishes *Roderick Hudson*, *A Passionate Pilgrim and Other Tales*, and *Transatlantic Sketches*.
1875–1876	Moves to Paris to write Paris letters for the *New York Tribune*. Befriends Ivan Turgenev and Charles Sanders Pierce, meets Gustave Flaubert, Edmond de Goncourt, Emile Zola, Alphonse Daudet, Guy de Maupassant, Ernest Renan, and Gustave Dore, and is not impressed by the early impressionists.
1876	Settles in London in December.
1877	Publishes *The American*, meets Robert Browning and George du Maurier, and visits Paris and Rome.
1878	Publishes *French Poets and Novelists*, "Daisy Miller"—which provides him with widespread fame on both sides of the Atlantic—"An International Episode," and *The Europeans*. Elected to the Reform Club and meets Alfred, Lord Tennyson, George Meredith, and James Whistler.
1879	Enjoys celebrity status and London society. Establishes friendships with Edmund Gosse and Robert Louis Stevenson and spends a great deal of time with Henry Adams. Publishes *Hawthorne*.
1880	Publishes *Washington Square*.

Chronology

1880–1881	Visits Florence, Paris, and Venice and earns an income of $500 a month.
1881	Publishes *The Portrait of a Lady*.
1881–1882	Revisits America and meets President Chester Arthur.
1882	Mother dies 29 January, followed by his father on 18 December. Quarrels with William over their father's will. Becomes a member of the Athenaeum Club and visits the dying Turgenev.
1883	Publishes *Siege of London* and *Portraits of Places*. Macmillan brings out a pocket edition of the novels and tales in 14 volumes. Prepares a stage version of "Daisy Miller." Wilky dies in November.
1884	Visits Paris and meets John Singer Sargent. Alice, suffering from a nervous disorder, comes to live near James in London. Publishes *Tales of Three Cities* and "The Art of Fiction."
1886	Publishes *The Bostonians* and *The Princess Casamassima*.
1886–1887	Enjoys an extended stay in Italy and spends much time with Constance Fenimore Woolson, the novelist and grandniece of James Fenimore Cooper.
1888	Publishes *The Reverberator, The Aspern Papers, Louisa Pallant, The Modern Warning*, and *Partial Portraits*. Continues to worry about his expanding waistline.
1889	Attends Browning's funeral. Publishes *A London Life*.
1889–1890	Dramatizes *The American*, visits Paris, Florence, and Venice, and begins to write a series of drawing-room comedies for the theater.
1890	Publishes *The Tragic Muse*.
1891	*The American* has a successful theatrical run, but James's comedies fail to find backing. Alice is diagnosed as having cancer. James Russell Lowell dies.
1892	Attends the funeral of Tennyson. Alice dies 6 March. Publishes *The Lesson of the Master*. *The American* continues to be performed.
1893	Fanny Kemble dies. Continues to write plays and publishes *The Real Thing and Other Tales*.
1894	Deeply shocked by the suicide of Constance Fenimore Woolson. Robert Louis Stevenson dies. Publishes *Theatricals: Two Comedies* and *Theatricals: Second Series*.
1895	*Guy Domville* opens in January to a hostile reception, occasioning his abandonment of the theater. Publishes *Terminations*.

1896	Publishes *Embarrassments*.
1897	Publishes *The Spoils of Poynton* and *What Maisy Knew*. Leases Lamb House, Rye, Sussex, where he is visited by Ford Madox Ford and establishes his friendship with Joseph Conrad. A painful wrist prompts him to begin dictating his work to a stenographer.
1898	Publishes "The Turn of the Screw" and *In the Cage*. Meets Stephen Crane and H. G. Wells.
1899	Visits Paris, Venice, and Rome. Sees his brother William for the first time in six years. Hires James B. Pinker as his literary agent. Purchases Lamb House for $10,000.
1900	Alternates between Rye and London.
1901	Sees the funeral of Queen Victoria. Meets George Gissing.
1902	Publishes *The Wings of the Dove*.
1903	Publishes *The Ambassadors*, *The Better Sort*, and *William Wetmore Story and His Friends*. Meets Edith Wharton.
1904	Publishes *The Golden Bowl*.
1904–1905	First visit to America after a 20-year absence. Meets President Theodore Roosevelt and travels and lectures extensively, delivering "The Lesson of Balzac" in Philadelphia and "The Question of Our Speech" at the 1905 Bryn Mawr commencement. Elected to the American Academy of Arts and Letters.
1906–1908	Writes 18 prefaces for the 24-volume New York edition of his works (published 1907–09).
1907	Visits Edith Wharton in Paris and travels to Italy for the last time. Publishes "The Jolly Corner" and *The American Scene*.
1909	Establishes contact with members of the Bloomsbury group and meets John Maynard Keynes at Cambridge. Begins friendship with Hugh Walpole. Destroys 40 years' worth of papers. Suffers from gout. Publishes *Italian Hours*.
1910	Suffers ill health and suspects a nervous breakdown. His remaining brothers, Rob and William, die in America, where James remains for the winter. Publishes *The Finer Grain* and *The Outcry*.
1911	Receives honorary degree from Harvard. Spends much time in London while beginning his autobiography.
1912	Receives honorary doctor of letters degree from Oxford. Sees much of Edith Wharton and meets André Gide. Ill health continues with shingles.

Chronology

1913   Sargent paints his portrait to mark his seventieth birthday. Publishes the first volume of his autobiography, *A Small Boy and Others*.

1914   Publishes the second volume of his autobiography, *Notes of a Son and Brother*, and *Notes on Novelists*. Appalled by World War I, James spends a great deal of time and energy in war relief projects.

1915   Continues war relief work. Meets Prime Minister Herbert Asquith and Winston Churchill. Granted British citizenship in July 1915. Burns more of his papers. Suffers two strokes in December and develops pneumonia.

1916   Awarded the Order of Merit on New Year's Day. Dies on 28 February. The funeral is held in Chelsea, and after his body is cremated, the ashes are buried in Cambridge, in the family plot.

Literary and Historical Context

1

Historical Context

Washington Square (1880) was written in 1879, at the end of a decade in which Henry James had spent much of his time traveling in Europe before finally settling in London in 1876. It is the final flourish of the apprentice work in *Roderick Hudson* (1875), *The American* (1877), and *The Europeans* (1878) and was composed with the confidence and fluency animated by the commercial and critical success of *Daisy Miller* in 1878. It is also, distinctly, a farewell to America as a scene for James's fictional action: certainly he would people his later novels with Americans, but it is rare to find them located outside Europe—*The Bostonians* (1886) is the only notable exception. And it is, finally, a peculiarity within James's oeuvre, a peculiarity in company with *The Europeans*: these are the only two works in which he chose to set his action in a distinct historical past. Both novels, written within a couple of years of each other, are located in the America (New York and New England, respectively) of the 1840s. Never again would James allow himself this backward glance.

   The historical context of *Washington Square* is most meaningf displayed through two principal areas—the development of the of the novel, and the changing nature of economic and mark tices. *Washington Square* inaugurated the shape of modern fiction and was conceived during that transitional moment when the modern economy began to emerge from its nineteenth-century forms. One of the great achievements of James's novel is to register the intimacy between aesthetic and commercial concerns at the crucial point where both assumed new outlines.

James's place in the history of the novel, a place graphed vividly by *Washington Square*, is at the meeting place between two distinct forms—the romantic, characteristic of American fiction, and the realistic, characteristic of European fiction. His place is a negotiation between the competing practices of the respective examplars, Nathaniel Hawthorne and Honoré de Balzac. The terms of that negotiation are best summarized in a famous contrast between the novel and the romance provided by Richard Chase in *The American Novel and Its Tradition* (1957). Chase, rightly, takes the main difference between the two to lie in the ways in which they view reality. The novel renders reality "closely and in comprehensive detail," depicting people in their "real complexity of temperament and motive" and "in explicable relation to nature, to each other, to their social class, to their own past." The world presented by the novel is, above all, recognizable and plausible, densely expressed, and filled with knowable detail. By contrast, the romance "feels free to render reality in less volume and detail"; action is less constrained by the visible world and encounters "less resistance from reality." Character does not depend upon "much intricacy of relation," whether to other characters, to society, or to the past. The "immediate rendition of reality" is not so urgent for the romance as it is for the novel; the former displays instead a tendency toward the abstract and the symbolic.[1]

The romance, then, is a much freer form, but it eschews the structures of social and historical density we associate with the novel. What James attempts is to test the possibilities of each within his negotiations of their respective practices: he wants, in *Washington Square*, both the *solidity* of realistic fiction and the *fluidity* of romantic play. I have chosen these latter terms carefully: they mark the ᵃcy between the new form of fiction we find in James and the ᵍ nature of contemporary commerce to which he responds.

Historical Context

The rapid industrial growth and the spread of corporations during Reconstruction engendered a vast increase not only in wealth but in change in the perception of the goods being produced. America's first industrial revolution through to the 1830s and 1840s, the period of the setting for *Washington Square*, operated on the notion that the value of an object was determined by its inherent properties. The second industrial revolution of the 1870s, the period of the novel's composition, recognized that value was to be determined more by the dictates of the marketplace, by the laws of supply and demand. Goods themselves were not the only subjects of this change: land, perhaps the most "solid" entity of all, became, in the hands of the developers and speculators, equally susceptible to the fluidity of the new economy. Ownership became recognized principally through documents rather than through productive labor, the documents matching the bank notes (at the expense of specie) and shares that measured the new corporate wealth. The shift was from solidity (of the inherent properties of goods or the productive labor of land) to fluidity (of market shifts or the uncertainties of speculation). What emerges is, with some literalness, a paper world—it is deeply instructive that one of the major political debates during the 1870s resuscitated the earlier anxieties of the 1830s and 1840s about the respective merits of coined and paper money, a debate that gives figure to these larger issues of solidity and fluidity.

The historical context of *Washington Square* is the concomitance of these aesthetic and economic considerations. Notions of solidity and fluidity inform both the new form of Jamesian fiction in its negotiation of the novel and the romance, and the movements of contemporary commerce. The solidity of Dr. Sloper (whose scientific temperament registers the valorization of technology during America's second industrial revolution), with its capacity for fixing things against change and movement, is visibly set against the fluidity of Morris Townsend, who mirrors all the mobility, novelty, and uncertaint of the changing world. Caught between them is Catherine, who victimized as the commodity in human form, paralyzed within instability of the marketplace. The major voice of the novel is a device that takes its literary impetus from the model of Jane

5

of presentation through the tone of conversation rather than through conversation's ostensible subject. Here, again, we find a reworking of the interplay between solidity and fluidity, between established meaning and the fluctuations of utterance. And here also we find a further way of reading *Washington Square*'s most immediate context—the story told to James by the actress Fanny Kemble upon which he based the action of his novel. The story about her brother's mercenary wooing of the plain daughter of the master of King's College, Cambridge, has a visibly English resonance, but James transposed it to America. In a letter of 8 June 1879, immediately prior to the composition of *Washington Square*, James observed that "the British mind is so totally un-ironical in relation to itself."[2] In his novel he deployed the tactics of irony in its American context as part of the new fictional form he forged from the interstices of his two principal literary traditions at a moment of striking material transformation.

2

The Importance of the Work

Broadly speaking, categories of importance may be subsumed under the significance of a text within a writer's complete oeuvre, within literary history at large, and, most urgently, within our estimations of the text's societal resonance—how it helps us to understand human relationships and to see the ways in which those relationships are constructed. It is within these general areas that the importance of *Washington Square* may be recognized.

The novel belongs to James's early period and clearly cannot lay claim to the emotional and technical sophistication of the later works (*The Ambassadors* [1903] or *The Wings of the Dove* [1902], for example), or even to the remarkable perceptiveness of the intervening works, such as *The Bostonians, The Princess Casamassima* (1886), or *The Awkward Age* (1899). These are the more accomplished affairs, but it is precisely in *Washington Square's* falling short of such accomplishment where we discover its significance—that is, in its *process* of exploration and experimentation. James is never the sort of writer in whom we find accomplishment as a finished thing, as an enclosed and enclosing "final" account of its preoccupations, but it is in his earlⁱ novels (*Washington Square* is exemplary here) where we witness *activity* of what Wallace Stevens, thinking of modern poetry, would later call "the act of finding / What will suffice."[1] In *Washington Square* this "act of finding" is the exploration of ways of representing American social history, an exploration that seeks new forms of fictional procedures. The text discovers these forms by negotiating, principally, the existing models of literary representation in the verisimilitude of European realism (where Balzac provides James's touchstone) and the imaginative leeway of the American romance (where James finds his main resource in Hawthorne). James's process of negotiation allows his social and historical preoccupations—the effects of America's rapidly developing commercial practices and the beginnings of the consumer culture—to be displayed in ways that would not be possible within either of his governing models conceived separately. In other words, the importance of *Washington Square* lies not simply in its radical restructuring of fictional form, but in its recognition of that form's capacity to give witness to the history that enables its production. The novel marks an extraordinary closeness between its thematic project and its aesthetic innovation.

That importance is amplified by the second half of Wallace Stevens's dictum. *Washington Square* registers not only an "act of finding" but an act of finding "What will suffice." Now *suffice* is a deliberately understated and unspectacular term for talking about literature, and as such, it directs us to the particularly American and the particularly modern nature of James's achievement. It proposes an aesthetic of adequacy—of language, character, and situation, of the standard *topoi* of fiction that are not allowed to foreground themselves with any bravura but are simply sufficient to their occasion. This modesty not only locates James's significant advance on his American literary predecessors and contemporaries—the cosmic catalogs of Walt Whitman, the metaphysical convolutions of Herman Melville, or the oblique landscapes of Hawthorne, for example—but it also captures exactly the tone of *Washington Square*: the tone of an emotionally restrained investigation into the fate of carefully observed individuals ᵃt a moment of historical change. It is a tone that eschews the colorful ᵈ dramatic expression we might otherwise expect to find in those ᵉ straightforwardly "realistic" representations of the subject. If one had to choose two terms that encapsulate, without being reductive, the importance of James's achievement in *Washington Square*, they would surely belong to the lexicon of *modesty* and *restraint* at the levels of conception, treatment, and preoccupation. James's skillful control of size within these vital areas of theme and representation is what provides potent resonance for the story of Catherine Sloper and her fate under America's commercial accelerations.

The presentation of Catherine's historical fate is the pinnacle of the novel's greatness. All too often, literary realism leaves its characters simply caught in the nexus of the social and economic circumstances that its authors portray with such painstaking verisimilitude. Catherine is certainly caught—but she is not trapped by the novelistic paraphernalia that can imprison the reader within the illusion of a realistically knowable world. James's strength here is to display his characters as a focus for the play of wider societal imperatives, but by refusing to express that play through "realistic" attention—here, the minutiae of the business world of lower Manhattan—he allows its more intimate, and human, effects to be seen more clearly. He reads between the lines, as it were, of the relationships between individuals and their society, and by resisting the direct expression of that society, he allows his reader also to read between the lines—to witness these effects in their more potent intrusions. The potency of such indirection is achieved by James's respect for the latitude he seeks both for his fiction and for its reader. Jamesian latitude is willing to exploit the forms of setting (institutions, cities, streets, rooms) that realism relies upon to exhibit social force, but it refuses any unquestioning comfort, of solidity, or familiarity, those forms may thereby endow. The issue is perhaps best summarized by a moment in James's *Hawthorne* (1879), a study of his most immediate literary predecessor that he wrote just prior to writing *Washington Square*. He is admiring Hawthorne's democratic sense by discriminating between the flexibility of American individualism and what he sees as the fixed nature of the communal standard whereby a European tends to judge: "The individual counts for r as it were, and thanks to the absence of a variety of social tyr settled heads under which he may be easily and convenientl holed, he is to a certain extent a wonder and a mystery. An E a Frenchman . . . judges quickly, easily, from his own social standpoint, and makes an end of it . . . and he has the advantage that his standards are fixed by the general consent of the society in which he lives."[2]

The project of *Washington Square* is exactly to release us from such quick and easy judgment, the judgment so often encouraged by realistic fiction. Catherine does indeed become a "wonder and a mystery," and her fate is meaningful because it is refused the expression of "general consent" and is prey to direct forces whose very directness allows us to feel that we know where we are and therefore that we may suspend proper interrogation of those forces. Her fate cannot be "pigeon-holed" by the "settled heads" under which, for example, Flaubert or Balzac consider their characters' vulnerability to society's machinations. The dialogue between the American romance and the European novel that is negotiated by James releases the new possibilities for fictional form that characterize his importance as a writer in general and guarantee the emotional potency of *Washington Square* in particular.

3

Critical Reception

James himself was not fond of *Washington Square*. He omitted it from the New York edition of his novels and tales a quarter of a century later, a fate shared by the bulk of his "American" work, including *The Europeans* and *The Bostonians*. We cannot estimate with any accuracy the reasons for James's subsequent dissatisfaction with the work he had chosen to set in America, but there is no doubt that critical commentaries have been powerfully guided in their choice of material by the inclusions and exclusions of the collected edition of 1907–09. This in part explains why the earlier novels, especially those that suffer the double burden of being set in James's home country, attracted relatively little attention from the critics. *The Europeans* and *Washington Square* in particular have been neglected. By comparison, *The Portrait of a Lady*, the novel that was much in James's mind whilst writing these other two, has prompted at least double the interest animated by the two together. Even at the moment of its composition Jam thought *Washington Square* a "poorish story" (Letters II, 268 "slender tale, of rather too narrow an interest" (Letters II, 308) pily, the novel attracted a more positive response from its rea It was the first of James's novels to be serialized in bot and America (in the *Cornhill* [June-November 1880] and in *Harper's* [July-December 1880], respectively), and the book edition was considered a "great success" by his publishers.[1]

However, the response of that more professional readership, the contemporary reviews, tended to be solemnly judgmental. The most substantial of these was a notice by R. H. Hutton in the *Spectator* for February 1881; he found the novel to be a "marvellously clever" study of a "leaden-coloured group of emotions": "There is no doubt that it is genius, and genius of the most marked order, genius for painting character, a genius for conceiving unalloyed dismalness of effect, without tragedy and without comedy. If you desire a consumately clever study of perfect dreariness, you have it in *Washington Square*" (quoted in Gard, 89, 90). Nineteenth-century seriousness would take a while to be able to read James with a more flexible understanding. An unsigned review in the *Literary World* for January 1881 matched the tone of Hutton's opinion in seeing the novel as a "clever bit of psychological anatomy" (quoted in Gard, 91), as did the anonymous commentator in the *Atlantic* for May 1881, who claimed that the wit and ingenuity of the novel was "almost its sole excuse for being" and sententiously urged, "If one presents himself the high problems of life for solution, he may be pardoned a little impatience over the elaborate nonentities who occupy the pages of *Washington Square*" (quoted in Gard, 92). Innovation is always difficult to appreciate contemporaneously, but the broad canvases upon which these reviewers attempted to accommodate the novel ("tragedy," "comedy," and "the high problems of life") are clearly too unwieldy for the modesty, understatement, and refusal of dramatic bravura that so richly characterize *Washington Square*.

Later in the century, when Jamesian subtlety had had more opportunity to restructure novelistic expectations, an unsigned article appeared in *Murrays's* for November 1891; it has been properly recognized as "one of the critical oases" in the reception of James's work (Gard, 221). Here, amid a recognition of James's artistry and an acknowledgment of his modernity, *Washington Square* is found worthy of comparison with Balzac's *Eugénie Grandet* (1833), a comparison that moves beyond the suburban prejudice against cleverness to recognize James's modernity within his historical and moral vision: "In historical accuracy and broad grasp of the foundations of life, there is no work with which the American novel can be so fitly mated as with that of the great French master" (quoted in Gard, 226). James himself saw his novel as "a tale purely American" (*Letters* II, 268), and this is a crucial clue not only to help us understand what the novel is about but to chart the shifts in its reputation.

Washington Square received "appreciative references" from a few critics during the early twentieth century (notably, Joseph Warren Beach, Van Wyck Brooks, and Pelham Edgar).[2] The most striking of these is Rebecca West's subtle recognition in 1916 of the understated, nondramatic tenor of James's presentation. She argues for the novel as a "work of great genius" in which James "concentrated all the sense which he had absorbed throughout his childhood of the simple, provincial life which went on behind the brown stone of old New York." She notes the "most deliberate cunning" with which he expresses "the woe of all those people to whom nothing ever happens, who are aware of the gay challenge of life but are prevented by something leaden in their substance from responding."[3] West's recognition of the special, and complex, ordinariness of the novel was not to be pursued in any detail until John Lucas did so in a highly perceptive essay nearly half a century later. It was not until Ezra Pound's great restoration of James in the *Little Review* of August 1918 (written at a time when James's general reputation was in decline) that we discover full acknowledgment of the historical force of James's Americanness. Pound negotiates James in company with French novelists—particularly Flaubert, whose dictum, if *L'Education sentimentale* [1869] had been read the Franco-Prussian War could have been averted, was one of his abiding aesthetic principles—and proposes James as, above all, a diagnostician, "so thoroughly a recorder of people, of their atmospheres, society, personality, setting."[4] Pound's reading marks a major advance in the critical reception of James: "As Armageddon has only too clearly shown, national qualities are the great gods of present and Henry James spent himself from the beginning in an a... sis of these potent chemicals . . . which chemicals too little reg... have in our time exploded for want of watching. They are manent and fundamental hostilities and incompatibles" (Pound, 300–301).

James as historian in this sense is a radically new James, and Pound, perhaps as a fellow exile who needed a degree of native reassurance, gives substantial admiration to the "social history" in James, which puts "America on the map"; Pound sees *Washington Square* (in company with *The Europeans*) as "so autochthonous, so authentic to the conditions" (Pound, 302). Pound's argument should be highlighted because, until recently, critics by and large have chosen not to read the historicist James, preferring instead the James of aloof and difficult artistry or the James of complex psychological perception. Such a critical climate has not been hospitable to *Washington Square*.

Serious academic attention to James remained rare until the 1940s. The exception was Cornelia Pulsifer Kelley's *The Early Development of Henry James* in 1930. Kelley claimed *Washington Square* as a "masterpiece" and was the first to give sustained consideration of the novel's debt to *Eugénie Grandet*, providing a good example of James's complex play with his sources and reminding us of one of James's most specific admirations for Balzac—the principles of good storytelling. Kelley is not sensitive to the novel's evocation of place ("Adequately done as a background, it is most inadequately done in itself") but praises the artistry of its "straightforward narrative," which abjures the use of a narrator or other perceiving consciousness to tell the story "as he saw it and not as one of his characters did."[5] Under the aegis of the New Criticism, commentators tended to focus upon James's later works, but F. O. Matthiessen managed to recognize in 1944 that, "despite its slightness," the novel "is so accurate in its human values that its omission from James's collected edition is the one most to be regretted."[6] More interestingly, three years later, in collecting James's American material, Matthiessen drew attention to James's own disquiet about his inability (circumscribed by his familial, ocial, and cultural circumstances) to portray what he called the own-town" workings of the business world.[7]

While James may have been ignorant of the practical details of orld, his texts are powerfully alert to its human effects. And, ntly, this awareness is not simply a matter of a particular body of knowledge or experience. As Matthiessen recognizes, it has also to do with James's wider sense of authorship—specifically, with the gender status of writing. Matthiessen allies the tacit place of the "downtown" to James's negotiation of the "extraordinary absence" of a "serious male interest" (*Novels and Stories*, xv). James's sense of authorship was of a feminized profession amid an insistently masculine world, and as Leon Edel makes plain in his biography, this sense in part explains James's choice of the betrayed female as his major protagonist in so much of his work.[8] Catherine Sloper is the first example of the many such heroines (rather than heroes) who are to follow. The issue of gender in James generally remained unacknowledged in the commentaries until the brilliant analyses of Alfred Habegger during the last decade,[9] but in 1978, on a narrower scale, Mary Doyle Springer sought to recognize the historical resonance of *Washington Square* by describing the place of the female within the society of its period. Springer's project was the first to give independent attention to Mrs. Penniman: "Aunt Penniman exists to reveal by her actions the real heart of the darkness: that in such a milieu women . . . not only cooperate passively with what the ethics of a paternalistic society makes necessary, but also cooperate actively in exploiting each other because that is what the whole social system gives them to do, and gives them little else to do if they are unmarried." And Springer accurately notes Mrs. Penniman's role: "to double our sense of how these women live, and by her silly actions and reactions to throw into relief the pathos and dignity of Catherine's actions and reactions."[10] This later observation contributes well to F. W. Dupee's sense of the novel's tactics, nearly 30 years previously: "Between victim and victimizer there is a human middle ground which Catherine makes her own."[11]

A good deal of the critical debate about *Washington Square* has interested itself in the novel's setting; attitudes have tended to be polarized. While F. R. Leavis argued in 1948 that "the New Yor[k] setting gives James an opportunity for such a record of the *moeurs* a past age as he alone should have done,"[12] and Edel in 1962 di[scov]ered in James's presentation of the Square "both a personal [and] historical symbol of American upper-class life" that testifie[s] destructive power of a materialism untouched by the im

TECHNICAL
LEARNING
POST OFF
BEAUFOF

(Edel, II:597). Dupee asserted in 1951: "It is not essential to *Washington Square* that its scene is American. The Old New York setting is lovely but insubstantial, an atmosphere and no more." Dupee understood also, however, that the novel has a "small subject" that James explores "to perfection," and that this subject is "an unmistakably psychological one" (Dupee, 63). The novel's psychological probings have attracted several of its most interesting readings. Edel observes: "In terms of his recent life she [Catherine] is an image of himself as victim of his brother's and America's failure to understand either his feelings or his career. Dr. Sloper would appear to be still another of James's fictional recreations of his brother: the William who had a medical degree and treated him and his work with sarcasm and contempt—the William who could love him and also spurn him" (Edel, II:596). The line established by Edel was widened in 1963 by Maxwell Geismar, who defines the "emotional fabric" of *Washington Square* as a "tangled skein of avarice and incest."[13] Geismar sees how the "love-hatred-jealousy pattern" of a "classic" father-daughter relation anticipated the "even more complex incestuous and oedipal" family relationships of James's later works, and how Catherine's "resolution" of "silent suffering and emotional repression, of self-sacrifice and abnegation," forecast the "typical Jamesian resolution to all the tangled affairs of life" (Geismar, 38–39). More recently, and more generally, James W. Gargano has documented the processes whereby Catherine acquires "selfhood and inner being,"[14] while Richard B. Hovey focuses upon Sloper to analyze the novel's concern with "the inward violence, the emotional greed, the hidden evil."[15]

Inevitably, critics have probed into the literary sources for *Washington Square*. It has been generally recognized that these are most powerfully to be found in Balzac, specifically in *Eugénie Grandet*, and in Hawthorne, as essays by Robert Emmet Long, Harold Schechter, ·nd Thaddeo K. Babiiha have shown.[16] Equally inevitably, such prob-~s, despite their local worthiness, have only a limited place in the ¹og of the novel's reception. Before moving on to the major discus-ᵢt is worth remembering that, on occasion, some of the most moments in that catalog have occurred not within the sub-ᵒnographs or in the essays that devote themselves entirely nder consideration, but in what are almost parentheses in more general discussions. We find important examples of such parentheses in L. C. Knights, who notes that Dr. Sloper's characteristic form of discourse, irony, is a "form of distancing" designed to "prevent communication" and to "dominate,"[17] and in Terry Eagleton, who sees how Sloper's propensity for totalization displaces him from concrete history (the changing nature of New York) through the "hunt for the single, secret principle which will transform experience into the cohesive intelligibility of an artefact."[18] The observations of Knights and Eagleton are recorded here not only for their donative nature but because they might easily slip through the net of a standard bibliography on *Washington Square*.

Any modern discussion of the novel must begin in 1960 with Richard Poirier. Poirier resists the notion that "characters can be given a public solidity without the evocation of their place within a traditionally mannered society or even within a nationality" and so argues that the novel is "in its basic situation a melodramatic fairy-tale, complete with characters who have archetypes in everyone's most rudimentary literary experience and imagination."[19] Hence, the "public status" of the characters is defined by the latter rather than the former. Among the most useful points to emerge from Poirier's account is his dissociation of one of the novel's principal problems—the relationship between the narrative voice and that of Sloper. For James, Catherine becomes a "free" character, while for her father she remains "fixed":

> It is best not to think of this novel as a melodrama, but to observe that in response to the experience which it includes Dr. Sloper becomes a melodramatist and James does not. . . . The scientific atitude, with its presumptions about the predictability of a course of events, necessarily leads to the melodrama when human beings refuse to imitate the logical hypotheses which are imposed upon them. . . . Melodrama is the voice of the scientific mind when its theories have been defied by facts, when it is raised in a very illogical protest against the freedom of what it had assumed it had fixed. (Poirier, 179)

Poirier's thesis has proved influential for subsequent argumen[...] Geismar usefully sees Catherine as a "sleeping-princess heroine" [...] is surrounded "by a wall of cash rather than fire" (Geismar but Peter Buitenhuis uses the "archetypal function" of the characters merely to sustain an argument for the unimportance of the novel's setting.[20] More perceptively, and intelligently, John Lucas notes how much of *Washington Square* is conducted through dialogue in which "everything that is said is controlled by the social tone, so that *what* is said is inseparable from *how* it's said."[21] Recognizing the novel as one of social relationships in the tradition inaugurated by Jane Austen, Lucas persuasively extends Poirier's position: "If characters *do* become like stock types in stage melodrama and fairy tale—and I agree that they do—it is because they see themselves called on to play parts created by their self-conscious awareness of what their society requires of them" (Lucas, 38–39). He then displays how "people are always being caught out in gestures, and their being so enables that subtle investigation of the gap between the act and the actuality which James manages so finely" (Lucas, 51). Lucas concludes that "the brilliance of James's novel depends on the way in which its comic surface is played off against the tragic events" (Lucas, 59). This play is understood also as belonging to the novel's thematic preoccupations, a "relentless and detailed study of very ordinary goings-on in a particular society" where life is, above all, "unspectacular, mundane" (Lucas, 40). Here, the play allows "nothing strident" to substitute for "its unruffled and sure study of circumstance, of context, of concatenation of cause and effect." Lucas, with considerable wisdom, ends with the observation, "It is the ordinariness which is so extraordinary about *Washington Square*" (Lucas, 59).

The work of Poirier and Lucas draws attention to the issue of style in the novel, an issue that also informs the final two essays among the best of recent discussions. In 1975 Millicent Bell examined James's explorations of a variety of styles—"those of the realist-historian, the ironist, the melodramatist, and the romantic fabulist"—to propose that in Catherine we are presented with "a style so mute and motionless as to be almost the surrender of style—a practical and intellectual 'innocence' which derives from an inability to employ any manner dictated by social or literary convention." Out of this stylistic conflict born a new style, "a new language of authenticity," which is "the k of imagination, of the creativity of her plain nature," a plainness marking her "triumph of silence."[22] Bell's excellent argument suggests that style is *the* subject of *Washington Square*, a suggestion pursued by Stuart Hutchinson, who proposes that, "in its self-consciousness about its form as a novel, *Washington Square* is revealed after all to be very much an American work."[23] Hutchinson's claim for James's self-consciousness as "American" belongs to his general case for the strategic uncertainties of nineteenth-century American fiction—the problematizing in Hawthorne and Melville, for example, of authority, authorship, character, and structure. "Nothing comes prepacked in a sustaining historical and social shape to an American writer" (Hutchinson, 59). And it is this self-consciousness that reveals *Washington Square* to be also "incipiently modernist" (Hutchinson, 11) in the sense that "James is also turning a critical eye on how he himself composes" (Hutchinson, 16).

The only other survey of the critical reception of *Washington Square* has been Darshan Singh Maini's 1979 centennial essay, and it is perhaps appropriate to conclude with a reworking of his conclusion: the novel "represents the earlier James just at the point in his development where the tutelage under French novelists is beginning to end. He has absorbed the lessons of the masters, and, within the borrowed form, a clear, new voice is heard" (Maini, 101). The French tutelage never ends for James, and the "new voice" would always maintain Balzac and Hawthorne in tandem to create through style a fresh way of acknowledging fiction's responsibilities to history and to society.

A Reading

4

A Peculiarly American Sense
of History

Washington Square is about history, about the ways in which economics and commercial practices structure human relationships, and about the ways in which history may be represented in fictional forms. Such a claim may look odd when applied to the work of a writer who has long been viewed by literary critics as somehow innocent of any but the most rarefied of feelings about his characters and situations and as unwilling (even unable) to recognize the more material forms of social intercourse and experience. I dispute these views, and I want to read *Washington Square* as part of that dispute by attending to its expression of James's historical sense.

My starting point lies in recognizing the curious status of *Washington Square* in the Jamesian canon. It is one of only two of his novels (the other being *The Europeans*, published two years previously in 1878) to be set in a discernible period of the past, and the setting is roughly the same for both—the America of the 1830s and 1840s. In other words, within the space of two years, and for the only time in his entire literary career, James chose to concern himself specifically with that phase in American history that witnessed the extraordinary development of industrial and commercial practices characterizing

America's first industrial revolution. Furthermore, it is not insignificant that *Washington Square* is the only novel for which James chose a specific locale for a title: historical time and geographical place are the issues that overtly confront the reader to an extent insisted upon as nowhere else in his works (excepting in the slightly later novels, *The Bostonians* and *The Princess Casamassima*).

With these singularities in mind, I want to investigate both the nature of James's return to a particular past from the position of the late 1870s and the historical sense that governs that return. It is an investigation that will need to advance a historical sense that differs from those forms of solidity and density, those accumulations of recognizable details, that we customarily associate with the historicity of realism in fiction. In many ways, most critics of James during the present century seem to take their cue on this issue from a famous 1918 essay by T. S. Eliot. Eliot compares James with Hawthorne and argues: "Both men had that sense of the past which is peculiarly American, but in Hawthorne this sense exercised itself in a grip on the past itself; in James, it is a sense of the sense."[1] Eliot's argument has a certain rightness to it: Hawthorne is more "solid" (Eliot's term) than James in his presentation of the manners and mores of his subjects and in his depictions of the locales of colonial life, but that is not the point. James begins *Washington Square* with a depiction of time that is strategically indeterminate: "During a portion of the first half of the present century, and more particularly during the latter part of it . . ."[2] James's indeterminacy here might lend weight to Eliot's accusation that he has "a sense of the sense," particularly if we compare the beginning of *Washington Square* with the opening to *The American* (1877), a slightly earlier novel: "On a brilliant day in May, in the year 1868. . . ."[3] While the latter tells us exactly where we are, the former gestures toward temporal specification with an air not so much of vagueness as of a deliberate blurring of the securities we seek through chronological time. In fact *Washington Square* plays a whole series of games with time in order, partly, to destabilize the comfort we seek in knowing exactly where we are (I shall return to these games at a more appropriate point later). Oddly enough, given the differences in their openings, *Washington Square* reveals a very clear sense of the past, while *The American* simply sets its action in what is effectively little more than the near present.

A large part of James's innovativeness as a writer is his urge for what he calls in "The Art of Fiction" (1884) the "air of reality"—the tone of the real without the accoutrements of literary realism, historical resonance without the itemized resources of history's events.[4] Eliot's thoughts on James in connection with Hawthorne turn out to be very useful in this respect because James's monograph on his literary ancestor contains much that is pertinent to the reading procedures we need to develop in responding to James's historicism. *Hawthorne* was published in 1879, immediately prior to the composition of *Washington Square*, and marks a moment when we discover James negotiating a different form of past, the past of literary history, in an attempt to structure his own future. As Tony Tanner has perceptively noted: "It is as though by 'placing' his great predecessor James was tentatively marking out the territory he intended to claim as his own."[5]

The key lesson in *Hawthorne* for my present argument lies in one of James's observations on the Civil War, which shadowed Hawthorne's final years: "When history herself is so hard at work, fiction has little left to say" (*Hawthorne*, 157). It is important to realize what James is *not* doing here. His position does not privilege "history" over "fiction" but rather recognizes that the two are not to be seen as competitive, that the experiences of life are not to be confused with those of art. This position has instructive consequences for the literary expressions of history. James finds in Hawthorne an absence of realism—that most obvious of literary devices for registering history, which James usually associates with the French practitioners of the novel, Balzac, Flaubert, and Zola—but does claim that his work is "intensely and vividly local" and "redolent of the social system in which he had his being" (*Hawthorne*, 23–25). Hence, "it cannot be too often repeated that Hawthorne was not a realist. He had a high sense of reality." James insists, from the evidence of Hawthorne's note books, that, "fond as he was of jotting down the items that make it up, he never attempted to render exactly or closely the actual facts of the society that surrounded him." Hawthorne's refusal of "actual facts" (to a degree, characteristic of James himself) engenders a radically different form of historical registration: "The reader must look for his local and national quality between the lines of his writing and in the *indirect* testimony of his tone, his accent, his temper, of his omissions and suppressions" (*Hawthorne*, 119). Such a reading and the writing to which it responds are peculiarly American: "An American reads between the lines—he completes the suggestions—he constructs a picture" (*Hawthorne*, 54).

Reading between the lines, being alert to the indirection of testimony, to omissions and suppressions, completing suggestions—these are the activities that we engage in as readers of *Washington Square*'s historicity. To suggest that these activities are derived solely from James's appropriation of Hawthorne is slightly misleading, because that appropriation is conducted through an awareness of those absences in Hawthorne that James finds fulfilled in the different resources of European realism, particularly in the work of Balzac. Throughout his career, James used the models of *both* the Balzac novel (filled with the "items" and "actual facts" of the social world that are refused by Hawthorne) and the Hawthorne romance (with its reliance on suggestiveness and indirection untrameled by the details of empirical social observation) as a means of negotiating his own special style, his own characteristic means of historical registration. The novel and the romance forms continually question, test, modify, and experiment with each other in James's work, but their relationship with each other is not solely a matter of style. The historical preoccupations of *Washington Square*—James's analysis of the bourgeois temperament exemplified in the figure of Dr. Sloper, and his casting of the novel's action back to the period of America's first industrial revolution from the position of the second great phase of commercial expansion in the 1870s—raise issues of human behavior within an accelerating economy that render the respective material and immaterial arenas of these styles of writing as deeply embedded within the social changes of half a century.

James always finds much to praise in Balzac's work—its solidity of specification, its extraordinarily detailed attention to situation and circumstance—but, with Hawthorne in mind, he finds also a real danger in the potentially imprisoning effects of those virtues: their capacity for confining both writer and reader by their very solidity and detail, leaving little room for maneuver, for imagining alternatives. Within a culture rapidly becoming structured as a marketplace, where social intercourse is increasingly measured and evaluated by a world of seemingly solid goods, these matters of style acquire an especially acute historical pertinence. While James is negotiating competing aesthetic concerns in *Washington Square*, he is, at the same time, experimenting with ways in which those concerns may register the contemporary history that is the novel's subject.

Millicent Bell has written well on the question of a literary "model" for James while he was writing *Washington Square*. The period 1878–79 seems, she rightly notes, "to have been pivotal in James's career, a time when Balzac's and all other models both teased and repelled." Illuminatingly, she suggests that it was, in part, a recognition of Balzac's inappropriateness that contributed to the shape of James's own procedures: "the use of a central consciousness whose confinement of scope was its interest." I would go further and argue that, for James in the late 1870s, Balzac and Hawthorne, with their differing, often mutually exclusive practices, were inseparable. As Bell herself notes, "If *Washington Square* derives from *Eugénie Grandet* it may also be said to come out of 'Rappaccini's Daughter' " (Bell 23–24). We might extend this perception to claim that, while the image of the dominant father we find in Dr. Sloper clearly belongs to both of these texts, the latter is more donative if only for the simple fact of Sloper's profession as a man of science. Hawthorne's fictions are well populated by scientific figures who are felt to be not only cruel with respect to human affections but arrogant in their distortions of nature: to Rappaccini we may add Aylmer, Ethan Brand, Dr. Heidegger, and Roger Chillingworth.[6] The business of amplifying "sources" does not belong to my present concern, which is to suggest that the debates about materiality and immateriality we find incorporated in the styles of Balzac and Hawthorne are essential not only for James's new ways of witnessing history but for the contemporary turmoil registered by *Washington Square*. However, I hope it is not too fanciful to suggest that while Sloper's house is conceived as a haven from the turbulence of lower Manhattan that becomes a prison for huma relations, so the miserly provincialism of *Eugénie Grandet* suggests a prison of style that is questioned by the more liberating possibilities of Hawthorne's tale. I choose the idea of liberation advisedly because it is the promise, on behalf of both writer and reader, of Hawthorne's notion of "latitude" that, as I shall suggest shortly, is essential to James's historicity. Initially, it is a liberation from that familiarity of the world we find as a major resource in the argument for novelistic realism, from that tangibility of a scene or situation that we are encouraged, rather unquestioningly, to assume we recognize. It is not accidental that Hawthorne chose to play with such liberation in "Rappaccini's Daughter" by inventing a thinly disguised pseudonym for his authorship ("From the Writings of Aubepine") and by prefacing the tale with an equally thinly disguised account of his own literary position. His game aims at liberation from overly solid perceptions of authorship, from confining notions of origin, by the very thinness of these disguises. The trick works by being palpably a trick whereby we are alerted to the disgrounding of authority that is to be a chief function of "latitude."

James plays a similar trick toward the beginning of *Washington Square*. We have already noted how the novel opens with a gesture of indeterminacy toward time, one of the basic properties of novelistic convention. Carefully placed at the very end of the first chapter is James's disruption of a further novelistic property—the voice that authorizes our reception of the narrative. The voice is disrupted in a way that confuses and disguises authorial utterance; it finishes with a recognizably Hawthornesque mysteriousness about its entire enterprise: "[Catherine] grew up a very robust and healthy child, and her father, as he looked at her, often *said to himself* that, such as she was, he at least need have no fear of losing her. *I say* 'such as she was,' because, to tell the truth—But this is a truth of which I will defer the telling" (WS, 30; my emphasis). James's trick here belongs to his general worries about novelistic conventions, summarized early in his writing life when he concluded his 1873 review of *Middlemarch* (1871–72) with a famous question: "It sets a limit, we think, to the development of the old-fashioned English novel. Its diffuseness . . . makes it too copious a dose of pure fiction. If we write novels so, how shall we write History?"[7] During the later years of his life, he was able to allay such worries by a faith in the dramatic "objectivity" he defines in his preface to *The Awkward Age*: "The divine distinction of the act of a play . . . was, I reasoned, in its special, its guarded objectivity. This objectivity, in turn, when achieving its ideal, came from the imposed absence of that 'going behind', to compass explanations and amplifications, to drag out odds and ends from the 'mere' storyteller's great property-shop of aids to illusion."[8]

James's skepticism about novelistic connections, his aversion to any pseudopsychological "going behind" and to the "property-shop of aids to illusion," tended in the years between these two statements, to express itself through his insistence on matters of technique. This insistence often relies upon a series of geometrical metaphors that marks a clear resistance to the material world by its advocation of the ideas of surface and relationship at the expense of novelistic furniture. It is one of James's greatest achievements as a novelist (and part of the history through which he writes), to recognize the social mask as the principal articulator of character. The mask is acknowledged as the surface through which social performance and relationship are engi-neered—not as a form of front or disguise that conceals some other order of truth or self, but as a new form of social reality occasioned by particular historical shifts. The social mask resists, above all, any illusory tendency toward "going behind" a character to reveal a more "realistic" nature. These preoccupations are especially vivid in *The Europeans*, the companion-piece to *Washington Square*, and, as I shall show, indicate an arena where matters of style are intimate with mat-ters of history.

James's geometrical metaphors, his advocation of character as surface, and his worries over novelistic procedures do not, as one might imagine that they do, present a reductive model wherein we read competing fictions of the real and the imagined. They do, how-ever, indicate James's willingness to confront the risk of alienating fiction as a social force, a willingness that derives from his interest in the complex of the novel-romance, the material-immaterial, presented by Balzac and Hawthorne. An excellent essay by Leo Bersani has attended to Jamesian geometry in order to read its distances and abstractness as providing more accurate witness than the conventional depth-led "going behind" of novelistic fiction:

> It's as if he came to feel that a kind of autonomous geometric pattern, in which the parts appeal for their value to nothing but their contributive place in the essentially abstract pattern, *is* the artist's more successful representation of life. . . . The only faithful picture of life in art is not in the choice of a significant subject (James always argued against that pseudorealistic prejudice), but rather in the illustration of sense—of design-making processes. James proves the novel's connection with life by deprecating its derivation from life; and it's when he is most abstractly articulating the growth of a structure that James is also most successfully defending the mimetic function of art (and of criticism).[9]

Understood in this sense, James's abstract geometry is a process of design, revealing the world as, above all, a manufactured place, made by human hands; design, conceived abstractly, will be of great help in our task of reading between the lines of James's fiction—a lesson he learned from Hawthorne. To read between the lines is James's way of reading history within its human effects and without the misleading habits of "going behind" that are encouraged by novelistic realism. Crucial here is that most pervasive of Jamesian subjects—freedom. It is to be apprehended, as Bersani puts it, "in the sense of inventions so coercive that they resist any attempt to enrich—or reduce—them with meaning"(Bersani, 57–58).

What is involved here is the principle of recomposition. The principle applies not only to James's own practice but to the liberty of both his characters and his readers, and as we shall see, it is essential to his presentation of history—a presentation wherein he refuses the novelistic confinement of those bare facts that provide such a potent resource for fiction conceived in naturalistic or realistic terms. To anticipate the argument that will follow, we might briefly exemplify this notion of presentation by considering James's choice of profession for Austin Sloper. Professions are always especially revealing in James's work, because of their rarity, and we might legitimately ask why Sloper is cast as a doctor. If my assertion is to have any accuracy—that the history presented by *Washington Square* is predominantly a history of economics and commercial expansion—then surely it would have been more expressive to have Sloper be a businessman of some kind? The answer would be yes if we were engaged with the fiction of Balzac and his contemporaries, or of William Dean Howells, Theodore Dreiser, and Frank Norris. James's recomposition involves a more oblique angle that eschews the directness of presentation we would find in these other writers. As we shall see, the characteristics associated with medicine (principally, balance and rationalism) are seen to be those that in less obvious, and hence less comforting, ways are also pertinent to the resources of commercial practice. Both belong to a similar epistemology, and the indirect testimony of James's presentation (another lesson from Hawthorne) will yield more fully the design of that epistemology and the intimacy of its intrusions upon social interaction.

James's sense of the design-making process, his endless analyses of his craft, his geometry of fictional and human behavior, must be seen as a means of exhibiting his own production—enabling his fictions to display their own process, to escape the realms of mystification (the realist or naturalist ambition for fiction to mirror life beyond itself), and to make themselves available for interventions, for recompositions, by others. By maintaining this possibility for recomposition, for imagining alternative worlds (again, a consequence of Hawthornesque "latitude"), James refuses to appropriate the freedom of his readers. He resists the potential of fiction to compete novelistically with a world that is solidly and confiningly familiar to us. His predilection for what he calls "that magnificent and masterly indirectness" stresses that what is necessary for fiction is not so much objects in themselves as the slant of vision that appropriates those objects. Liberty in style and in behavior are thus equally guaranteed by obliquity of angle, by expression rather than description. There is a great deal at stake here: notions of freedom are closely bound up with styles of writing—with recomposition and the imagining of alternatives—that reconstruct the presentation of history.

Such reconstruction is discovered in the lessons of the Hawthornesque romance considered against the realistic-naturalistic practices of the novel (particularly in its French forms) that predicate a direct and didactic mimesis. Hawthorne's preface to *The House of the Seven Gables* (1851) establishes its "moral" as a cry against the impositions of one generation upon another; he continues by wishing not "relentlessly to impale the story with its moral as an iron rod— or, rather, as by sticking a pin through a butterfly—thus at once depriving it of life, and causing it to stiffen in an ungainly and unnatural attitude." In distinguishing between the forms of the romance and the novel, he calls this authorial freedom "latitude," and he extends it to readers in warning them against "that inflexible and exceedingly dangerous species of criticism" that attempts to bring "his fancy pictures almost into positive contact with the realities of the moment." Hawthorne insists that the worlds of fiction and experience are not in competition with each other in order to achieve an effect of "laying out a street that infringes upon nobody's private rights."[10]

It is this "latitude" that James has in mind in claiming that Hawthorne was "not a realist" but was possessed of "a high sense of reality" that "never attempted to render exactly or closely the actual facts of the society that surrounded him" (*Hawthorne*, 119). James is referring here to the superabundance of the items that constitute "realism" in Hawthorne's notebooks. Although in his own notebooks the reverse is true, the effect is the same, as Taylor Stoehr has noted: "The notebooks in which James stored his materials are filled with plots and the making of plots—relationships, encounters, sketches of action. There is little interest in facts or truths observed from life, and the stories he hears at dinner-parties are chiefly regarded as 'germs' for his imagination to work with, the less of the actuality known the better."[11] By the time he wrote his prefaces (1906–08) to the New York edition, James was capable of being coy about even his "germs" (the closest he ever comes to "facts")—of which he makes great play at the beginning of his preface to *The Awkward Age*—but nevertheless, the notebooks, more so than his published essays, provide good evidence of his interest in the pattern, the design of things prior to the more familiar statements in the prefaces. The result is a sense of how "reality" might be offered without the rhetoric of realism, detectable "between the lines" of writing, in "indirect testimony" (*Hawthorne*, 119).

A Peculiarly American Sense of History

In considering the "finest thing" in *The Blithedale Romance* (1852)—the character of Zenobia, "the nearest approach that Hawthorne has made to the complete creation of a person"—James remembers Hawthorne's warning against too close an identification between the characters of fiction and persons of experienced life—in this instance, the critic and reformer Margaret Fuller: "There is no strictness in the representation by novelists of persons who have struck them in life, and there can in the nature of things be none. From the moment the imagination takes a hand in the game, the inevitable tendency is to divergence, to following what may be called new scents" (*Hawthorne*, 127). Divergence is another means of advocating recomposition; it is probably not a coincidence that within a few years (1885) James would engage in a vigorous debate with his brother William in which he disavowed the imputed resemblance between the fictional Miss Birdseye in *The Bostonians* (which, along with *The Princess Casamassima*, was James's fullest exploration of the possibilities of realist fiction, and which had as one of its most immediate literary antecedents *The Blithedale Romance*) and Hawthorne's sister-in-law, Elizabeth Peabody.[12] James's view of characters who might be assumed to enjoy some degree of affinity with recognizable persons is a good example, on a local scale, of how recomposition and historical obliquity work at the practical level—what he calls, in his essay "Alphonse Daudet" (1883), the "delicacy" whereby a painter "conjures away recognition" (*French Writers*, 235). And it must be remembered that this Hawthornesque, romantic line in James is often considered in relation to what it resists in the principles of realism. His observation on Zenobia does not prevent him from simultaneously admiring the presentation of the narrator in *The Blithedale Romance*, a character whose standpoint has "the advantage of being a concrete one" and who is "no longer, as in the preceding tales, a disembodied spirit, imprisoned in the haunted chamber of his own contemplations," but "a particular man, with a certain human grossness" (*Hawthorne*, 126). In other words, James is responding positively to flesh-and-blood characterization here, a palpable solidity that alerts him to one of the dangers in Hawthorne—the danger of disembodiment, which is always a potential consequence of obliquity pursued too rigorously and which may always be modified by the Balzacian detail. James recognizes this danger in employing the rhetoric of realism itself to make his final judgment on *The Blithedale Romance*. He reproaches the story for failing to avail itself of "so excellent an opportunity for describing unhackneyed specimens of human nature," so that we "get too much out of reality, and cease to feel beneath our feet the firm ground of an appeal to our own vision of the world, our observation." The "brethren of Brook Farm" may well have regretted, James suggests, that Hawthorne "should have treated their institution mainly as a perch for starting upon an imaginative flight" (*Hawthorne*, 129).

The positions expressed in the preceding paragraph are all assumed in the study of Hawthorne, published by James immediately prior to his composition of *Washington Square*, in which he describes the America of the 1840s, the period of most of the story's action, as "given up to a great material prosperity, a homely *bourgeois* activity," as a place where among the "cultivated classes" was found "much relish for the utterances of a writer who would help one to take a picturesque view of one's internal possibilities, and to find in the landscape of the soul all sorts of fine sunrise and moonlight effects" (*Hawthorne*, 88). This is a complicated statement, not least because it is difficult to estimate the extent of James's irony, expressed as it is with a degree of warmth, or at least, of understanding. The "picturesque" is an important term within James's aesthetic vocabulary at this point in his career; it is central to his conception of the "fun" he explores in *The Europeans*, for example, and it is usually intended as a liberating device for the imagining of alternatives. At the same time, it carries here undeniable suggestions of bourgeois escapism. In *Washington Square* it largely defines Mrs. Penniman's theatrical response to the bourgeois world that comfortably encloses her and in which her all-pervasive "sense of the picturesque" endows her with a "natural disposition to embellish any subject that she touched" (*WS*, 187). Hers is a drama that drastically fails the great Jamesian test of discrimination; it is played out on a stage on which "the idea of last partings occupied a place inferior in dignity only to that of first meetings" (*WS*, 178). Her refusal of difference and her predilection for embellishment remove her from the material world of process and change just as much as does the rationalistic scientism of Dr. Sloper: both tend toward the reification that seeks to render the world immutable. It is difficult to imagine Mrs. Penniman as a reader of Hawthorne, but her capacity for the "picturesque" provides a starting point for noting the entanglement of James's study with his novel's temporal location and its bourgeois characteristics. At the least, she offers a good example of the dangers within the romance in her distance from "the firm ground of an appeal to our own vision of the world." James's sense of both the limits and the extent of the romance and novel forms points up the interstitial field of *Washington Square* and the insubstantiality that it risks.

It was while James was working on *Washington Square* that his *Hawthorne* "created its storm in the American press" (Edel, I: 595). The "storm" attacked James for losing his native point of view, for his "foreign" and arrogantly deprecatory treatment of Hawthorne, and for what was seen as an emphasis on the parochial and provincial quality of American society (*Edel*, I: 586–90). There is no doubt that the preoccupations of the novel are informed by this "storm," and that the "storm" casts further light on the complex of the romance-novel that, I have been urging, is determinant for James's presentation of history. One of the few concrete remarks James made about *Washington Square* was in his reply to Howells's review of *Hawthorne*: he describes it as "a tale purely American, the writing of which made me feel acutely the want of the 'paraphernalia' " (*Letters II*, 268). That "paraphernalia" is Howells's term for the "items of high civilisation" that James had listed as absent from American life and that had occasioned so much criticism in the American press:

> The negative side of the spectacle on which Hawthorne looked out, in his contemplative saunterings and reveries, might, indeed, with a little ingenuity, be made almost ludicrous; one might enumerate the items of high civilisation, as it exists in other countries, which are absent from the texture of American life, until it should become a wonder to know what was left. No State, in the European sense of the word, and indeed barely a specific national name. No sovereign, no court, no personal loyalty, no aristocracy, no church, no clergy, no army, no diplomatic service, no country gentlemen, no palaces, no castles, nor manors, nor old country-houses, nor parsonages, nor thatched cottages nor ivied ruins; no cathedrals, nor abbeys, nor little Norman churches; no great universities nor public

schools—no Oxford, nor Eton, nor Harrow; no literature, no novels, no museums, no pictures, no political society, no sporting class—no Epsom nor Ascot! (*Hawthorne, 55*).

James's reply (alert, perhaps, to the potentially "ludicrous" tenor of his "ingenuity") recodes these "items" within their more general categories, which constitute a writer's material—"manners, customs, usages, habits, forms"—and maintains their realist provenance: "I shall feel refuted only when we have produced . . . a gentleman who strikes me as a novelist—as belonging to the company of Balzac and Thackeray" (*Letters II*, 268). However, in *Hawthorne* itself, James's "items" belong to a more complicated notion of composition whereby the realistic and the romantic are not to be so conveniently separated. On the page preceding his list, he quotes from the preface to *The Marble Faun* (1860), the only novel that Hawthorne set outside America: "No author, without a trial, can conceive of the difficulty of writing a romance about a country where there is no shadow, no antiquity, no mystery, no picturesque and gloomy wrong, nor anything but a commonplace prosperity, in broad and simple daylight, as is happily the case with my dear native land" (*Hawthorne, 54*). The "items" James provides are thus, in the first instance, designed to enumerate the resources unavailable to Hawthorne, what James, thinking of Hawthorne's *American Notebooks*—seen by James as "a practical commentary upon this somewhat ominous text [*The Marble Faun*]" and characterized by "an extraordinary blankness" despite the author's "large and healthy appetite for detail"—refers to as "the lightness of the diet to which his observation was condemned" (*Hawthorne, 54*). But James's quotation erases the awkwardness of Hawthorne's statement, leaving it as an apparently uncomplicated disposition of a "broad and simple daylight" against the absence of "shadow" and "antiquity." His erasure is effected by deleting the sentences surrounding the quotation, sentences that, commenting on the suitability of Italy as a setting for *The Marble Faun*, set "a sort of poetic or fairy precinct, where actualities would not be so terribly insisted upon as they are, and must needs be, in America," against the proposition that "Romance and poetry, like ivy, lichens and wallflowers, need Ruin to make them grow."[13]

Hawthorne's position in this preface is by no means straightforward, and it is part of the function of James's erasure to render it reductively for the sake of his wider argument, which will restore its complications in James's own terms. While he is not sure that Hawthorne "had ever heard of Realism," he finds it "not fanciful" to suggest that Hawthorne "testifies to the sentiments of the society in which he flourished almost as pertinently (proportions observed) as Balzac and some of his descendants—MM. Flaubert and Zola—testify to the manners and morals of the French people" (*Hawthorne*, 24). James's choice of the term *testify* is particularly expressive of the new kind of realism he is trying to coax out of the complex of Hawthorne-Balzac, romance-novel: it suggests a "giving witness to" and belongs to the vocabulary of registration that he will use pervasively for his definitions of the writer's function. Strategically, it is not the familiar language of mimesis and diagnosis, which would be more usual for contemporary realism. His placing of Hawthorne in this company occurs within a page of a famous passage that suggests that his catalog of "items" is precisely a catalog of rhetorical resources (what Howells's review of *Hawthorne* termed "those novelistic 'properties' ")[14] rather than cultural condemnation. The passage points up the "valuable moral" James derives from Hawthorne, a "moral" that suggests the invidiousness of "contrasting his proportions with those of a great civilisation": "This moral is that the flower of art blooms only where the soil is deep, that it takes a great deal of history to produce a little literature, that it needs a complex social machinery to set a writer in motion." This is, however, only half of the "moral"—the half to which critics so often attend in isolation—and, too easily, it might seem to match the later comment on the absence of resources for the American writer. The gritty practicality of the second half firmly modifies any impulse to make such a match: "American civilisation has hitherto had other things to do than to produce flowers, and before giving birth to writers it has wisely occupied itself with providing something for them to write about." The sturdiness of James's recognition here, wonderfully undermining the metaphor of the first half of the "moral," suggests how he is able to see Hawthorne, "in spite of the absence of the realistic quality," as "intensely and vividly local" (*Hawthorne*, 23). Furthermore, James would appropriate such localism for his own purposes by reconstituting the conventions of realism.

James's appropriations of Hawthorne, particularly in his thoughts about *The House of the Seven Gables*, extend beyond his need to disorientate the comfort of established categories of writing, and beyond even his insistence on possibilities for the reader's flexibility. The liberty proclaimed by Hawthorne's preface in the "moral" he cautiously offers for the story, and in the "latitude" he wishes his form to maintain, enables James to describe him as "an American of Americans," which he defines by noting that, despite a sense of Hawthorne's conservatism, "it is singular how often one encounters in his writings some expression of mistrust of old houses, old institutions, long lines of descent" (*Hawthorne*, 123–24). Hawthorne's "moral"—"the folly of tumbling down an avalanche of ill-gotten gold, or real estate, on the heads of an unfortunate posterity, thereby to maim and crush them" (*Gables*, 2)—thus parallels the "latitude" he claims for his authority as a writer and for the reader, whom that authority inevitably threatens to maim. The debate about the ownership of property that constitutes the story itself elaborates this intersection of imaginative and material liberty. Brook Thomas has a good argument that is helpful here. It is premised on the American political system's founding on eighteenth-century models of impersonal authority, freed from subjective interests and justified by natural law. He claims:

> The status given a deed of property confirms the idea that an owner's authority to possess land is embodied in a text. A deed allows the person whose name is affixed to it to claim ownership of a piece of land. In a sense the document and the piece of property merge. The owner of the deed is the owner of the land. . . . But Hawthorne is acutely aware that sign and signifier do not coincide. Texts—including legal documents—have human authors and therefore derive their authority from human actions, not natural law. Furthermore, a document may as easily come from the irrational area of imagination as from the rational.

Thus, for Thomas, Hawthorne's story "questions the impersonal, rational authority of a democracy's most sacred texts—its legal documents.">[15] Hawthorne's questioning of texts, of the authority of writing itself, is, then, simultaneously a questioning of a material ideology. His questioning is enabled through the "latitude" he seeks in the romance form, and it is within the intersection of these concerns that his preoccupation with his own means of expression in the preface needs to be read.

It is also within this intersection that we need to read James's view of Hawthorne in the late 1870s—the time of *Washington Square*'s alertness to the impositions of a bourgeois economy, an alertness that my present exercise intends to document. Possession of property is the most material form of appropriation, of confining the freedom of others, particularly within a political system largely defined from the start by Lockean epistemology. The evanescence of portrayal practiced by Hawthorne (the object of both admiration and disquiet by James) itself resists the materiality that is the clearest product of such impersonal rationality. Impersonal rationality shares the guarantee of concealed authorship, fiction's suppression of its human agency; both are advertised as free from the excesses of the individual subjective imagination. Hence both most appropriately rely upon the rhetoric of realism, the nomenclature not only of politics and law but also of science (the major sanction for realistic fiction's self-advertisement), which derives its authority from the same rationality. While Hawthorne's Judge Pyncheon is an appropriator of property, James's Dr. Sloper is an appropriator of linguistic capital.

It has been the purpose of the present chapter to delineate the shape of the historical sense James developed at the time of *Hawthorne* and *Washington Square*, a shape that was prompted by the strengths and weaknesses he detected in the possibilities of Hawthorne and Balzac considered simultaneously. The interference between those possibilities is what constitutes the newness and the difficulty of James's view of society and history—a view that requires, at bottom, solidity of representation without its potential for confinement. While I have been stressing the "latitude" advocated by Hawthorne as the most effective means of resisting confinement, we should not forget that James never lost his admiration for the Balzacian fact. This aesthetic debate would become profoundly embedded within the history to which *Washington Square* provides testimony—the history of economics and commercial expansion, a history that is itself bound up with the issues of the material and the immaterial raised by James's artistic probings.

In a local sense, we can see what is happening at the aesthetic level by noting how the novel disfigures its immediate source. James's "germ" for the story was provided by his friend, the actress Fanny Kemble, who told him of the mercenary courtship by her brother Henry Kemble of Mary Thackeray, the daughter of George Thackeray, the master of King's College, Cambridge. The father disapproved of Henry's suit and threatened to cut her off if marriage ensued. Henry discontinued the courtship, much to the distress of Mary, who chose to remain a spinster for the rest of her life. James's notebook entry (21 February 1879) recording the "germ" pays virtually no attention to the father and concentrates instead upon the selfishness of the young man, neglecting even the girl's misery.[16] What is interesting here is not so much the differences of attention between the notebook entry and the novel (such differences are unavoidable through the process of composition), but how James "conjures away" the story's "real" provenance—its English setting. This conjuring away involves more than the proclamation James makes at virtually the same time in *Hawthorne* on the business of representing people who have struck one in real life: "The inevitable tendency is to divergence, to following what may be called new scents" (*Hawthorne*, 127). The setting is not simply transposed: the Americanness of its New York setting is, unusually for James, strongly present in his "truly American" story. Ezra Pound, James's poetic descendant, in his masterly 1918 essay, expands his judgment of the novel as "one of his best" by recognizing that it put "America on the map" in providing "a real past, a real background." Pound goes so far as to find it, in these terms, worthy of the company of *The American Scene* (1907), James's late record of his return to America in 1904–05 after a 20-year absence. Pound sees the latter work as "a creation of America. A book no 'serious American' will neglect." As an effort toward "a realization of that country," Pound claims to know of "no such grave record, of no such attempt at faithful portrayal." And Pound conjoins not only *Washington Square* but also its companion-piece, *The Europeans*, with *The American Scene* as bulking large in "the very small amount of writing which can be counted as history of *moeurs contemporaines*, of national habit of our time and of the two or three generations preceding us" (Pound, 312, 327). The French term here directs us back to the lexicon of the French realist novel practiced by Balzac and Flaubert and so reminds us of James's project in his deployment of the Hawthorne-Balzac complex, where we find a conjuring away of recognition combined with the authenticity of *moeurs contemporaines*.

My intention, then, is to recognize the historicity of *Washington Square* in its "indirect testimony"—that is, to read between its lines as it conjures away the conventions of realism in order to reconstruct them on behalf of, and from within, the processes of contemporary commercial and economic change. This will involve a return to my original question: the question of why James chose, uniquely in the late 1870s, to set the action of both *Washington Square* and *The Europeans* in the America of the 1830s and 1840s. My interest will focus on the development of the commodity relationship—understood as one of the major characteristics of the bourgeois culture of both periods—and on the subsequent effects of that relationship upon social manners and behavior.

5

Time, Place, and Balance

The time of *Washington Square* is, predominantly, the difficult period of the late 1830s and early 1840s. The opening three chapters of the novel (totaling 14 pages), prior to the beginning of the story's action in chapter 4, stress the period in which the novel is set to a degree that is unusual for James. Chapter 1 contains nine references to specific dates and to the ages of the characters, and chapters 2 and 3 each contain eight such references. The time scale marks one of those novelistic conventions that, as I shall show later, James is concerned to disturb.

The place of *Washington Square* is that area of lower Manhattan that awkwardly bastions itself against contemporary turbulence. Dr. Sloper's deliberate choices of residence are carefully located within a changing landscape. His first "edifice of red brick," within five minutes' walk of City Hall just north of Wall Street, "saw its best days" in about 1820, after which "the tide of fashion began to set steadily northward, as, indeed, in New York, thanks to the narrow channel in which it flows, it is obliged to do, and the great hum of traffic rolled farther to the right and left of Broadway." He moves north to Washington Square in 1835, when "the murmur of trade had become a mighty uproar" and when neighboring houses had been converted into "offices, warehouses, and shipping agencies, and otherwise applied to the base uses of commerce" (*WS*, 38–39).

Sloper's choices parallel the period of Manhattan's most rapid expansion, during which the island below Canal Street became condensed with overwhelming commercial activity. As Douglas T. Miller tells us: "The city was compact, extending from the southernmost point at the Battery north along the Hudson for about two miles and along the East River for approximately two and a half miles. Canal Street marked the northern limit in the late 1820s; beyond that were several separate villages—Greenwich, Chelsea, Bloomingdale, Manhattanville, and Harlem—and scattered farms and elegant country seats." At this time, "all was hustle and bustle in the metropolis; everything was given over to business and speculation" as New York became "the undisputed commercial center of the New World."[1] This pressure was topographically initiated by the reconstruction of the Wall Street area after the fire of 1835, the year of Sloper's move to Washington Square on the outskirts of the commercial district. The two decades between the Wall Street crises of 1837 and 1857 witnessed an extraordinary economic growth (Miller, 113), and in terms of the output of goods, the decade 1844–54, which covers most of the novel's action, was only slightly behind that of 1874–84,[2] the decade that instigated the "Gilded Age" and from which James composed the novel. The opening up of new markets was greatly aided by investment in the railways (Miller, 114–15), whose advancement signaled the development of a *national* economy and the transformation from self-sufficient farming and craft production to industrial manufacture and the factory system (Miller, 116, 118). Crucially, what Edward Pessen calls the "speculative spirit" of the mid-1830s and 1840s provided the capital support for technology in changing the hitherto local nature of the commercial system on behalf of a national market.[3]

This speculative urge points up one of the key factors in the changing commercial practice—its anonymity, figured by the emergence of the merchant capitalist as a necessary and dominant participant in the financing of industry (Pessen, 114), by the trend toward concentrating production in larger units controlled by absentee owners, and by the laws of incorporation (Miller, 107, 120). The corporate system inevitably encouraged the disengagement of owner and work force, particularly as, by the late 1840s, the organization of the stock market made stock speculation, which is wholly removed from the practice of production, an acceptable means to wealth. The stock market not only contributed to the anonymity of a developing capital-intensive economy but played a decisive role in blurring the divisions between "old" and "new" wealth, a process that inevitably expressed itself through the *embourgeoisement* of earlier hierarchies (Miller, 80).

Sloper's choice of location in Washington Square is an attempt both to retreat from the city's turbulence and to resist it, a means (characteristic of the bourgeois mind) whereby material process may be forgotten or obliterated. Peter Conrad's view of the novel's geography unproblematically sees this choice as an "occlusion of the city and the sanctification of an interior to shelter the private life."[4] Such a view is accurate enough as far as it goes, but it makes no attempt to discern the imperatives for "occlusion." Grievances against industrialism, the shifts to the factory system, the diminished value of labor, and the exploitative tactics of the corporate structure sought their expressions in the forms of social disorder.[5] In *The Great Riots of New York 1712–1873*, a book published in 1873—two years prior to James's departure for Europe, and six years prior to the composition of *Washington Square*—Joel Tyler Headley presented a historical explanation of the Draft Riots of 1863 and the Orange Riots of 1870 and 1871 that included substantial discussion of the unrest during the 1830s and 1840s. The prevailing fear of disorder was summarized by the New York *Commercial Advertiser* in August 1840: "Destructive rascality stalks at large in our streets and public places, at all times of the day and night, with none to make it afraid; mobs assemble deliberately . . . in a word, lawless violence and fury have full dominion over us whenever it pleases them to rage." In 1834, the year before Sloper's move to Washington Square, civil disturbances were so frequent that the year "was long remembered in New York history as the year of the riots."[6]

The brief voice of the changing city in *Washington Square* is Morris Townsend's cousin, Arthur Townsend, who, as a "stout young stockbroker," is the voice of the distanced power structure of a market economy that provides an accurate picture of living within the city's transformations: "At the end of three or four years we'll move. That's the way to live in New York—to move every three or four years. Then you always get the last thing. It's because the city's growing so quick— you've got to keep up with it." It is a picture strongly colored by a fascination with household gadgetry—domestic versions of the technology that creates the ground for wider economic and social changes: "So you see we'll always have a new house; it's a great advantage to have a new house; you get all the latest improvements. They invent everything all over again about every five years, and it's a great thing to keep up with the new things. I always try to keep up with the new things of every kind" (WS, 50). Townsend's abbreviated syntax and limited vocabulary are a telling Jamesian indictment. His reiteration of "things" suggests both an abstractive imagination and a reliance upon the stasis of reification.

Sloper's house, claiming the resistance of an "ideal of quiet and genteel retirement," paradoxically shares this modernity: it embodies "the last results of architectural science" (WS, 39) and was built in 1835, when Washington Square had become a fashionable address with its new neoclassic houses. But the narrative disguises this newness. James reminds the reader that he is proposing a retrospective history with the warm glow of a backward glance and claims that this part of New York "appears to many persons the most delectable" because of its "established repose" and its "riper, richer, more honourable look than any of the upper ramifications of the great longitudinal thoroughfare." He underlines his proposal by itemizing the area's "repose" through acts of familial memory. It is given a history as the place where "your grandmother lived, in venerable solitude," dispensing hospitality to "the infant imagination and the infant palate," where "you took your first walks abroad" and "your first school" was kept by "a broad-bosomed, broad-based old lady with a ferule, who was always having tea in a blue cup, with a saucer that didn't match." These memories are ingenuously foregrounded as a "topographical parenthesis," and they deliberately fudge the conditions of history by their naturalistic coloring and their association with the idea that the area expressed "the look of having had something of a social history" (*WS*, 39–40). Since Sloper's move to the Square occurs virtually at its nascence, it could exhibit such a "look" only from the retrospect of the later 1870s, the period of the novel's composition.

James's dispersal of time belongs in part to his tactic of removal from what he finds distasteful in the early manifestations of the Gilded Age, but more important, it exposes the extent to which he is liable to become enmeshed within the practices the novel sets out to criticize. He offers the Square as available to nostalgic recollection in order to play with his means of presentation, using the vocabulary of domestic memory, which we know derives from the past of his own family. This is the only place in the novel where such vocabulary appears, and it emphasizes itself as a warning against the elisions whereby nostalgia and memory discolor the experience of history.

Topographically, the Square performs a clear balancing act. Any map will show how it is placed in the border area that divides the rather narrow and crooked streets in lower Manhattan from the beginnings of the broad, geometrically precise avenues to the north of the old city. The balance is between the concrete names of the streets and the abstract numbers of the avenues. This topographical equilibrium is substantiated by the physical solidity of Sloper's house, "a handsome, modern, wide-fronted house, with a big balcony before the drawing-room windows, and a flight of white marble steps ascending to a portal which was also faced with white marble" (*WS*, 39). Sloper's solidity is intensified by comparison with the only other two domiciles described in the story, those belonging to his sisters, both of which are characterized by a locational vagueness. Mrs. Almond's house is, loosely, "much farther up town, in an embryonic street, with a high number," in a region where "the city began to assume a theoretical air," a region characterized by a long-vanished "rural picturesqueness" (*WS*, 40). Mrs. Montgomery's "neat little house of red brick" (which "has now disappeared"), out on the eastern edge of Manhattan, at least enjoys the limited specificity of being somewhere on Second Avenue; but it "looked like a magnified baby-house" that "might have been taken down from a shelf in a toy-shop" (*WS*, 96).

In the record of his return to New York in 1904, James would bemoan the avenues' mathematical expression of what he saw as the city's meanness—their expression of "her old inconceivably bourgeois scheme of composition and distribution."[7] The mathematical regularity of New York's grid may thus be seen as a display of bourgeois "consistency," straining to contain the energies of its commercial transformations in another version of balance. The idea of balance rationalizes the mathematical tenor of the bourgeois temperament, informing both the location of the Square and the scientific attitude of Sloper himself as he lives through the birth of corporate capitalism.

The opening page of *Washington Square* establishes Sloper and his profession by an elaborate configuration that, stylistically and thematically, assumes a variety of balances. As a definition of the medical profession, we are introduced to the epithet "liberal," which is explained by a further series of definitions drawn from the social realm of its operations. The first of these is a generalized judgment on the way value is ascribed: America is offered as "a country in which, to play a social part, you must either earn your income or make believe that you earn it." Such a "make-believe" strikingly anticipates Thorstein Veblen's *The Theory of the Leisure Class* (1899), one of the nineteenth century's major accounts of middle- and upper-class responses to the consumer culture that began to structure American life so powerfully during the Gilded Age. It would be no exaggeration to say that Veblen's text portrays with considerable accuracy the manners and mores of the world from which James wrote not only *Washington Square* but the bulk of his fiction. James's make-believe of earning an income foreshadows Veblen's recognition of how what he calls "the instinct of workmanship" comes to replace the standard of "conspicuous leisure" as a means of determining repute and value within the shifts of a consumer culture. This "instinct" relies precisely on the make-believe of display, expressing itself "not so much in insistence on substantial usefulness as in an abiding sense of the odiousness and aesthetic impossibility of what is obviously futile."[8]

The bourgeois system thus confers honor by means of a travestied purposefulness, a travesty that itself is occasioned by one of the major features of corporate practice—the visibly increasing divisions between intellectual and manual labor. Within this system, James's presentation of medicine claims the epithet of "liberal" by virtue of combining "two recognised sources of credit." It "belongs to the realm of the practical" (a version of manual labor), and it is "touched by the light of science" (a version of intellectual labor). The "healing art" is thus extended beyond medicine to the realm of "healing" literally—joining together the great schism of the bourgeois economy. Such healing is its social advertisement of itself, its particular make-believe. Hence, "it was an element in Doctor Sloper's reputation that his learning and his skill were very evenly balanced." This thematic balance is then mimed syntactically in the instruction, "To play a social part, you must *either* earn your income *or* make believe that you earn it" (my emphasis). The device of either-or has been explained in its negative formulation by Roland Barthes as one of the rhetorical strategies whereby the bourgeois habitually figures the world. Again, it is a balancing device, "a sort of intellectual equilibrium based on recognised places" whereby conflicting positions are anesthetized, relieved of their specific weight and balanced out in order to immobilize choice, to freeze proper, dialogical opposition.[9] The immobilization of choice will be precisely the fate of Catherine in Sloper's hands. And given that the form of balance I am advancing belongs to notions of impersonal, rational authority, it is entirely appropriate that Sloper's feelings for his wife were determined above all by his sense that she was a "reasonable" woman who exemplified his "idea of the beauty of *reason*" (*WS*, 32).

The explicitness of the axioms James uses to encode the medical profession now tends to disappear. It is replaced in the succeeding sentences by a syntactical balance of expression implicitly summoning Barthes's "figure of the scales" (his picture for "balance") into its utterance. For convenience, this syntactical balance is best illustrated by my emphases:

> He was what you might call a scholarly doctor, and *yet* there was nothing abstract in his remedies—he always ordered you to take something. *Though* he was felt to be extremely thorough, he was not uncomfortably theoretic; *and if* he sometimes explained matters rather more minutely than might seem of use to the patient, he never

48

went so far . . . as to trust to explanation alone, *but* always left behind him an inscrutable prescription. There were some doctors that left the prescription without offering any explanation at all; and he did not belong to that class *either*, which was after all the most vulgar. (*WS*, 27)

Sloper's "inscrutable prescription" is a good index to the relationship of his particular temperament with the world, a relationship characterized by the distances assumed in the precepts of mathematics and science, the governing codes for his temperament. The inscrutability of his prescription points up the vacancy of its subject, occurring as it does at the end of a series of propositions whose balance unites increasingly disparate subjects primarily by a syntax of negation. Both Sloper and his profession are circumscribed by omission rather than by social plenitude.

It matters that Sloper's profession is that of doctor, a man of science. The fact that he is not a businessman or a broker is, as I suggested in chapter 4, an illuminating instance of James conjuring away stable and comfortable positions: his diagnosis in *Washington Square* of contemporary commerce will be more accurately served by this oblique angle, which will recognize more substantially the schema of ideas authorizing business behavior and its human effects. It matters also that Sloper's profession is so conceived to reflect a period that experienced the determinant moments of radical economic change— the nascence of corporate modes of production and their subsequent enabling of the development of a consumer culture. Consistently throughout the novel we are reminded of the "light of science" by which Sloper views the world. The most fruitful example occurs in a conversation with Mrs. Almond that begins with a joke about geometry. Sloper gives his conviction that Catherine will "stick" with Morris Townsend, and Mrs. Almond asks, "Shall you not relent?" The conversation then runs:

> "Shall a geometrical proposition relent? I am not so superficial."
> "Doesn't geometry treat of surfaces?" asked Mrs. Almond. . . .

"Yes, but it treats of them profoundly. Catherine and her young
man are my surfaces; I have taken their measure." (*WS*, 137)

Sloper goes on in a more prosaic manner to talk as a chemist, one
of several versions of his insistence throughout that he wishes to ob-
serve the "mixture" of the case in question in order to see the "third
element" it produces (*WS*, 138). His analogy of "surfaces" and the
"geometrical proposition" is especially rich, partly because it exhibits
so clearly the tenets of Sloper's epistemology (his stance of the objective
scientist observing an experiment), and partly because it has such an
extensive and donative role in James's own critical theorizing and
fictional practices. As a general principle, "surface" is usually conceived as a social habit that is damaging when manipulated as a barrier
against positive human intercourse (usually for the purpose of some
sort of gain) and is ameliatory when employed as a device for increasing the possibilities of contact *with* the world. These issues were especially urgent for James at the time of writing *Washington Square*:
we see them explored in the novel that immediately precedes it, *The
Europeans*, and in the novel that so preoccupied his thoughts during
its composition, *The Portrait of a Lady*, and exemplified, respectively,
in the characters of Eugenia Munster and Serena Merle. The idea at
play here is that of social performativeness, recognized in the second
half of the nineteenth century as the new reality of a consumer culture.
I shall return to this performativeness and its historical provenance
when I discuss the role of Morris Townsend, but we may note in
advance that while the displays and gambits, the social masks or surfaces, of Eugenia Munster are designed to expand and enrich the range
of human contact, those of Serena Merle are restrictive and deadening.
It is clear that Sloper belongs to the latter category with its atten-
dant promise of protective and exploitative distance. His assumption
of the chemist's role in his continuation of the conversation about
geometry with Mrs. Almond is not solely a matter of dehumanized
behavior but, crucially, a reflex of economic history. Bourgeois balance
fixates the world, transforms history into essential types in order to
obscure, following Barthes, the "ceaseless making of the world." The
"motionless beam" that is bourgeois man—who, paradoxically, bases

his power on science's promise of unlimited transformation—balances out potential disruptions to render nature as "unchangeable" and "ineffable" (Barthes, 155, 141–42). Mathematics provides the main vocabulary for such balance. The work of Alfred Sohn-Rethel has demonstrated that mathematics contributes to the abstractions of an "ineffable" nature because it is the only "symbol language" that is capable of freeing itself from human activity. It thus registers not only the bourgeois disengagement from the material, changeable world, but also the divisions between intellectual and manual labor that are particularly exposed and exploited by the pressures of a developing market economy.[10]

The practices of scientific experiment and commercial enterprise are interlocked by a shared form of abstractive isolation that disguises material process. The abstraction shared by laboratory and factory is characteristic of the network of exchange itself, producing a "knowledge of nature in commodity form" (Sohn-Rethel, 132). The abstraction of commodities within the market is most clearly seen during their exchange, when their use-value is suspended, paradoxically frozen in the material world of their real production. Sohn-Rethel summarizes the point in a brilliant paragraph:

> There, in the market place and in shop-windows, things stand still. They are under the spell of one activity only; to change owners. They stand there waiting to be sold. While they are there for exchange they are not there for use. A commodity marked out at a definite price, for instance, is looked upon as being frozen to absolute immutability throughout the time during which the price remains unaltered. And the spell does not only bind the doings of man. Even nature herself is supposed to abstain from any ravages in the body of this commodity and to hold her breath, as it were, for the sake of this social business of man. (Sohn-Rethel, 25)

The commodity abstraction thus described belongs to the order of things whereby balance fixates the "making of the world" and the "types" of scientific positivism immobilize their objects. Abstraction, balance, and type all rely on a fetish of the already-made, the completed object that disguises its production, its memory of its own manufacture. All three share the paralysis of the "homogeneity, continuity and emptiness of all natural and material content" whereby time and space (the very coordinates with which *Washington Square* begins) are denied their capacity for differentiation in favor of "absolute historical timelessness and universality" (Sohn-Rethel, 48–49). The defeat of history and difference by assumptions of timelessness and universality involves further a denial of possibilities for human intervention—for materially altering the world conceived in terms of fixed objects that are authorized by custom, organization, or institution. The abstraction of commodities is part of their fixed status, visibly refusing their potential for use in the interests of exchange.

Finally, all three operate as a form of equivalence that achieves its most concentrated representation in cardinal numbers and in money, whose function, similarly, is to provide uniform shape for contradictory social relations. Hence, Sohn-Rethel finds the emergence of mathematical reasoning at "the historical stage at which commodity exchange becomes the agent of social synthesis, a point in time marked by the introduction and circulation of coined money" (Sohn-Rethel, 49, 47). It is not accidental that the periods of *Washington Square* (the 1830s–1840s of its setting and the 1870s of its composition) shared, as I shall document, a continuing debate about the forms of money itself—a debate that belongs not only to the changing shapes of manners and social performance consequent upon the development of a consumer culture, but also to the imperatives for James's notions of writing and presentation. Catherine, the principal victim of this combination of forces, will come to display their effects as a version of the commodified object herself.

6

Time, Place, and Money

James's interest in Hawthorne is in a writer who concerned himself with, as it were, the disguised histories of the real through his recompositions of the relationship between the imagination and felt experience, texts and con–texts, words and deeds. These recompositions suggest that we need to think of the moment of *Washington Square* in terms of the key issue that dominated both those periods of accelerated commercial expansion occasioning its action and its composition. This is the issue of money: specifically, the debates about "soft" and "hard" money, paper and coin, that prompted such intense public interest at the end of the Jacksonian era and during Reconstruction. By maintaining the tensile relationship between competing modes of style in *Hawthorne* and in *Washington Square*, the connections and disconnections between the rhetorics of romance and realism, James is involved in an aesthetic arena that is especially appropriate to the field where debates about coined and paper money were conducted. Both art and money raise the questions of symbolism and representation in general, the relation of words and signs to the objects, the immaterial to the material. James's displacements of style and the dematerialized center of the novel's action (its progressive diffusion of the specifics of time and place with which it begins)both belong to the instability in the hurly-burly of the commercial world. The main expression of that world—money—is shown to be notoriously uncertain of its own status as a result of its competing forms in coin and paper.

James's principal indictment of the bourgeois economy is found in the notions of rationalistic balance he expresses through the scientism of Sloper. It is the balance described by Roland Barthes as an "intellectual equilibrium based on recognized places" whereby "reality is first reduced to analogues; then it is weighed; finally, equality having been ascertained, it is got rid of." It is here that "one flees from an intolerable reality, reducing it to two opposites which balance each other only inasmuch as they are purely formal, relieved of all their specific weight." Material process, "reality," is erased in favor of a "final equilibrium" that "immobilizes values, life, destiny" so that "one no longer needs to choose, but only to endorse" (Barthes, 152–53). Theodor Adorno and Max Horkheimer have productively defined the bourgeois temperament thus: "Bourgeois Society is ruled by equivalence. It makes the dissimilar comparable by reducing it to abstract quantities." Such "equivalence" is seen to "dominate bourgeois justice and commodity exchange" as a form of abstraction. Abstraction characterizes the exchange relation of commodities (their existence to be no more than purchased), the determining objects of the bourgeois world. It also characterizes the distortive function of the main feature whereby the bourgeois is advertised, so that "the bourgeois ideal of naturalness intends not amorphous nature, but the virtuous mean."[1] Strikingly, one of the more problematical terms in *Washington Square* is *natural* as it is applied, predominantly, to Morris Townsend. As we shall see, James's analysis of the "natural" performativeness of Townsend raises one of the nineteenth century's most pervasive anxieties—the question of the self, its construction, and its social meaning.

I suggested earlier that Sloper is offered as a man of science rather than as a man of business because the latter would be too reductive an invitation to enjoin fictional and realist comparisons. It would also elide the nexus of relationships that make possible the fuller history of corporate market practice: relationships between abstract thought, rationalistic balance, numbers, science, technology, and industry. Furthermore, the etymological relation between the *species* and *specimens* of scientific inquiry and the *specie* of the money debates enables James obliquely to suggest the linguistic and ideological arenas in which he is willing to operate. Their shared Latin root means "appearance," so that both belong to an epistemology that relies on the "form," the "look" of its objects at the risk of an unstable or distorting distance from the assumed "reality" of those objects. And in another, closely related context, such a "form" clearly has a role to play in the performance of the "surface" or "social mask" that becomes newly valuable, and newly "real," for the display of the self within a consumer culture. Paradoxically, in common usage both *species* and *specie* acquire a strong empirical solidity and specificity.

The questions concerning representation raised by James's structuring of the Hawthorne-Balzac complex, by his acknowledgment of the performative self as opposed to an essentialist self (explored through the characters of Morris Townsend, Eugenia Munster, and Serena Merle), and by the money debates, thus circumscribe an area in which our faith about the truth of our means of expression and exchange is to be tested through an interplay of aesthetics, ontology, and money. All three crucially incorporate questions about freedom. I shall leave the issue of the self and its performative surfaces until my discussion of Townsend. Here, I want to consider the interplay between aesthetics and money. My starting point is an argument by Marc Shell, who is thinking about Poe's "The Gold Bug," a story of the early 1840s, the period of *Washington Square*:

> Credit or belief involves the very ground of aesthetic experience, and the same medium that seems to confer it in fiduciary money (bank-notes) and in scriptural money (created by the process of book-keeping) also seems to confer it in literature. That medium is writing. The apparently diabolical "interplay of money and mere writing to a point where the two become confused" involves a general ideological development: the tendency of paper money to distort our "natural" understanding of the relationship between symbols and things.[2]

The possibility of dis-credit, the gap between sign and signified, is thus a danger for both writing and financial speculation. James is interested in that gap as it characterizes the abstractions within the system of exchange but also as a resource for writing that requires the real without the rhetoric of realism, that insists on the imaginative liberty of alternatives. The proximity of these interests will lead us to the risks and, simultaneously, the accuracy of a historical sense that reads between the lines, that provides indirect testimony.

As Shell acknowledges, "America was the historical birthplace of widespread paper money in the Western World, and a debate about coined and paper money dominated American political discourse from 1825 to 1845" (Shell, 15). It was a debate that expressed itself most clearly in the political sphere through the argument about the banks and their appropriation of power. One of the best commentators on the issue, James Roger Sharp, has emphasized its politicization, claiming that, "to Jackson and his hard-money followers, banks occupied privileged positions in society and exercised tremendous and virtually unchecked power," and that "in an age dominated by an egalitarian spirit, the banks symbolized aristocratic privilege on the one hand, and the rapid and uncomfortable transition the country was undergoing from an agrarian to a commercial society on the other hand."[3] Sharp also argues—and this is vital for the historical positioning of *Washington Square*—that the bank debate reflected a wider argument about money that permeated the entire century: the rhetoric and fears of the Jacksonians mirrored those of the early nineteenth century expressed by John Taylor of Caroline—the clearest and most persuasive exponent of Jeffersonian principles, always the ground for the century's agrarian argument—and anticipated those of the Populist leaders toward its end. Their respective positions are summarized by the claim that "all were representatives of an agrarian society who felt that their moral values were being eroded away by the commercialization of society and the quickening tempo of industry" (Sharp, 6). So by the time of the Gilded Age the money issue focused the political rhetoric of the Populists just as acutely as it had that of the Jacksonians: "Throughout the century there was a fervently held belief that privately issued paper money was an exploitative device by which capitalists and bankers could control prices and the money supply. This, in turn, it was argued, gave these special citizens enormous political and economic power and made a mockery of a society that emphasized equal rights for all and special privileges for none" (Sharp, 8).

The mania for land speculation during the 1830s was made possible to a great extent by the absence of a *national* paper currency; the circulating medium consisted of specie and the paper money issued by the hundreds of local banks. The Jacksonians, in attempting to control the inevitable instability that accompanied (and, indeed, in large part enabled) such speculation, viewed the banks as a threat to an advertisedly free and democratic society and maintained a faith in specie as "a kind of perpetual and infallible balance wheel, regulating the workings of the banking system." Specie, they felt, had "an intrinsic and independent value of its own and could not depreciate as could paper money" (Sharp, 18). The uncertain symbolism of paper money was countered by an argument for the seemingly more solid symbolism of gold and silver, thus engendering the paradox of one form of abstraction competing with another on the contradictory grounds of its supposedly "natural" materiality.

William Leggett, in a well-known 1834 essay entitled "Equality," categorically places the issue in terms of class struggle—the dominance that inhibits the freedom of others: "The scrip nobility of this Republic have adopted towards the free people of this Republic the same language which the feudal barons and the despot who contested with them the power of oppressing the people used towards their serfs and villains, as they were opprobriously called." Throughout, Leggett opposes what he variously terms "would-be lordlings of the Paper Dynasty" and "phantoms of the paper system" to the "class which labours with its own hands." He displays here a clear application of the abstractions and distances based on a differentiation between intellectual and manual labor, a differentiation whose consequences became vividly apparent with the shift from agrarian to industrial practice and the developing conditions of commodity production and consumption. The former group was constituted by those whose "soul is wrapped up in a certificate of scrip or a bank note," and the only enemy facing the "labouring classes" was the "monopoly and a great paper system that grinds them to the dust."[4]

President Jackson utilized the same opposition in his Farewell Address of 1837: "The agricultural, the mechanical, and the labouring classes have little or no share in the direction of the great moneyed corporations."[5] Jackson's speeches in the 1830s exhibit succinctly the rhetoric of opposition to the questions of banks in general and paper money in particular. They elaborate a powerful equation between banks, paper money, and the abuse of democratic rights, along with manifest opportunity for fraud. At the very beginning of his "Bank Veto" address to Congress in 1832, Jackson stressed "the belief that some of the powers and privileges possessed by the existing bank are unauthorised by the constitution, subversive of the rights of the States, and dangerous to the liberties of the people."[6] His Fifth Annual Message (1833) reiterated the warning of constitutional infringement by offering what he termed "unquestionable proof" that the Bank of the United States had been converted into a "permanent electioneering machine," proof he used as a justification for his removal of the bank's deposits: "In this point of the case, the question is distinctly presented, whether the people of the United States are to govern through representatives chosen by their unbiased suffrages, or whether the money and power of a great corporation are to be secretly exerted to influence their judgement, and control their decisions."[7]

The instability of money's representation characterized the 1830s through its consequences: speculation and inflation. To control both, the Jackson administration issued in 1836 the "Specie Circular," which provided that only gold and silver could be accepted by government agents for public lands, the object of the most intense speculation by the middle of the decade. Such was Jackson's distrust of the possibilities for making something out of nothing that he chose to devote virtually the whole of his Farewell Address of 1837 to the question of currency. Arguably, it is the single most sustained attack, in a public document, on the "evil" of paper money, and the most rigorous justification of the "constitutional currency" of gold and silver. Jackson began by stressing the instability of contemporary conditions engendered by the untrustworthy symbolism of the paper medium:

> The paper system being founded on public confidence and having of itself no intrinsic value, it is liable to great and sudden fluctuations, thereby rendering property insecure and the wages of labour unsteady and uncertain. The corporations which create the paper money can not be relied upon to keep the circulating medium uni-

form in amount. In times of prosperity, when confidence is high, they are tempted by the prospect of gain or by the influence of those who hope to profit by it to extend their issues of paper beyond the bounds of discretion and the reasonable demands of business; and when these issues have been pushed on from day to day, until public confidence is at length shaken, then a reaction takes place, and they immediately withdraw the credits they have given, suddenly curtail their issues, and produce an unexpected and ruinous contraction of the circulating medium, which is felt by the whole community. ("Farewell", 154–155)

The "ebbs and flows" of the currency "naturally" engender a "wild spirit of speculation," which is morally harmful because it diverts attention from "the sober pursuits of honest industry" and fosters an "eager desire to amass wealth without labour." The temptation to create something out of nothing "inevitably" leads to an undermining of "free institutions" and a corruption of authority by locating power in the hands of a privileged few. Jackson's sense of currency's impoverished symbolism, made particularly expressive in the obvious dangers of counterfeit notes, encouraged him to frame his argument in terms of dominance and class:

> Some of the evils which arise from this system of paper press with peculiar hardship upon the class of society least able to bear it. A portion of this currency frequently becomes depreciated or worthless, and all of it is easily counterfeited in such a manner as to require peculiar skill and much experience to distinguish the counterfeit from the genuine note. These frauds are most generally perpetrated in the smaller notes, which are used in the daily transactions of ordinary business, and the losses occasioned by them are commonly thrown upon the labouring classes of society, whose situation and pursuits put it out of their power to guard themselves from these impositions, and where daily wages are necessary for their subsistence. ("Farewell", 155)

Such counterfeits encroach upon human freedom by the "natural associations" of the paper money system: "monopoly and exclusive privileges" ("Farewell," 157).

The debates about money during the 1830s (the period in which Dr. Sloper architecturally appropriates a portion of New York land to resist the city's accelerating commerce) thus marks a coalition of a series of social and aesthetic questions concerning the nature of symbolism and representation, their material referents and their consequent roles in redefined understandings about the nature of power and liberty. Political interest in the forms of money was revived during the years of Reconstruction and the Gilded Age, particularly during the 1870s, the decade that James ended with *Hawthorne, The Europeans,* and *Washington Square,* and the decade that, compared with the 1830s, experienced massive change in general, which Jan Dietrichson has usefully summarized: "The Gilded Age, the period from the end of the Civil War until about 1890, was a time of transition, of vast changes in American economic, social, and cultural life, when a new industrial and urban society emerged out of the older, predominantly agricultural and rural one. It is fair to say that this was the most radical transformation in the history of the nation."[8] Jay Martin has itemized the details of this transformation more specifically: "Rapid increasing wealth, the rise of the city, expanding immigration, a widened spirit of reform, mass education, a new scientific point of view, and the acceptance of technology as the American way of life—these were the interests that modified, contradicted, or merged with each other in American culture during the period between the wars."[9] Throughout the period of all these changes, it is money and its forms that provide the clearest index to the complex structure of the transforming world from which James was writing. The list provided by Jay Martin suggests material for the realist, Balzacian novel. By contrast, the debate about money that conjoins the periods of *Washington Square's* setting and composition suggests the oblique testimony James learned from the Hawthornesque romance. At the same time, it provides a base of sufficient solidity to obviate the danger of the social "blankness" he recognized in the latter form. In other words, it is not the "realism" of "rapid increasing wealth" that gives historical testimony to *Washington Square,* but, rather, it is the range of issues raised by the debate over the forms of money—forms that more intimately restructured human manners and behavior during the last quarter of the nineteenth century.

Time, Place, and Money

The Coinage Act of February 1873 (labeled the "crime of '73" by latter-day Jacksonians) put an end to the standard silver dollar. This demonetization of silver in effect redefined "coin" as gold and added considerably to the size of taxes. The Specie Resumption Act of early 1875 deflected the currency until it was at a par with gold. These acts were seen by the Populists as conferring a privileged monopoly on the banks, which, in Walter T. K. Nugent's words, "drew interest in gold on the government bonds the banks bought, and interest a second time on the notes the banks were then empowered to create and lend."[10] And the money question itself became paramount during the remainder of the decade, which experienced one of the country's worst depressions: "No one realized in 1865, but money was destined to become the chief perennial issue in national politics for over thirty years. . . . Its peculiar dimensions were established in almost all important ways during the Reconstruction years, from 1867 to 1879" (Nugent, 21–22). Richard Hofstadter extends the claim to argue for its symbolic resonance: "A whole generation of Americans were embroiled from the 1870s to the 1890s in the argument over silver. To the combatants of that era, silver and gold were not merely precious metals but precious symbols, the very substance of creeds and faiths which continued long afterward to have meaning for men living on the echoes of nineteenth-century orthodoxies."[11] Irwin Unger, in one of the best discussions of the subject, summarizes it succinctly: "In the decade and a half following Appomattox, national finance absorbed more of the country's intellectual and political energy than any other public question except Reconstruction."[12]

A statement in support of silver against gold by Congressman Richard Bland (Dem.-Mo.) in August 1876 reveals the extent to which the Reconstruction debate on "soft" versus "hard" money continued the rhetoric of the 1830s. Bland was speaking on behalf of a bill to remonetize silver, which he urged as "a measure in the interest of the honest yeomanry of this country." He saw the Public Credit Act of 1869 and the Coinage Act of 1873 as being wholly in the interests of "stock-jobbers and speculators." These acts promised payment of government bonds in coin rather than the paper currency with which they were originally purchased, and then redefined "coin" to be gold alone at the expense of silver. To argue that the taxpayer must pay

only in gold was "robbery, nothing more, nothing less," since creditors
would benefit enormously to the detriment of debtors:

> Because a measure is for once reported to this Congress that has
> within it a provision for the welfare of the people of the country
> against the corrupt legislation that has gone on here for the last
> sixteen years in the interest of the moneyed lords, it is here de-
> nounced as full of rascalities. . . . Mr. Speaker, the common people
> of the country cannot come to this Capitol. They are not here in
> your lobby. They are at home following the plough, cultivating the
> soil, or working in their workshops. It is the silvern and golden
> slippers of the money kings, the bankers and financiers, whose step
> is heard in these lobbies and who rule the finances of the country
> (quoted in Nugent, 96–97).

To Bland's catalog of dominating moneyed interests, we might
add the expansion of the corporate device during Reconstruction.
Dietrichson has claimed: "In use before the Civil War mainly as a
means to accumulate capital for turnpikes, railroads, and banks, the
corporation rapidly became the dominant force of business organization in the post-war years. . . . It gave continuity of control, easy
expansion of capital, concentration of administrative authority, diffusion of responsibility, and the privileges and immunities of a 'person'
in law and in interstate activities" (Dietrichson, 11). Such abstractive
"diffusion of responsibility" and "immunities" would have been
anathema to James, who always hated institutional or organized intrusions into private liberties. It is instructive that the only novels he wrote
that explicitly advertise a social history, *The Bostonians* (usefully, from
the point of view of *Washington Square*, set in the 1870s) and *The
Princess Casamassima* are each concerned with the impositions by
organizations—of feminists and of anarchists, respectively—upon personal freedom. James's concern extends to language. Taylor Stoehr,
on behalf of *The Princess Casamassima*, paraphrases an argument
from *The Theories of Anarchy and Law* (1887) by James's friend
Henry B. Brewster: "Man must learn to enjoy this freedom from settled
formulations. He must accept the responsibility for creating reality
through speech, and must refrain from the fetishism of names that

embalms life with words" (Stoehr, 130). Diagrammatically here, we have James's negotiation of Hawthorne and Balzac, the romance and the novel—albeit in somewhat reductive form since the issue is never so clearly presentable to James. In a paradoxical way, we might want to consider Verena Tarant's "natural" and "spontaneous" oratory in *The Bostonians* as belonging to the same field as the quietude that characterizes Catherine Sloper. Both are made subject to the pressures of abstract organization. Verena's voice is offered as a form of pure utterance whose contents are rendered vacuous by the rhetoric of Olive Chancellor's privileged ideals, while Catherine's vocal reticence is frozen by the impositions of her father. Catherine's quietude and Verena's utterance are equally emptied of material process and paralyzed by domestic versions of institutions.

Richard Bland's statement to Congress relied for its effect upon the full complex of ideas we associate with the Jacksonian position: the symbolism of money, the concentration of power and the consequent limiting of free voice and free action, and the division (admittedly nostalgic in expression) between intellectual labor (the paper world of the speculators) and manual labor (the concrete productivity of soil and workshop). The opposition of notes and specie during the earlier period had become recomposed into an opposition of silver and gold, but we should not assume that, within this recomposition, the apparent materiality of silver coin presented a more satisfactory symbolism than the obviously immaterial bank note. Coinage also figures as an abstract form of representation, as Alfred Sohn-Rethel has argued: "A coin has stamped upon its body that it is to serve as a means of exchange and not as an object of use. . . . Its physical matter has visibly become a mere carrier of its social function. A coin, therefore, is a thing which conforms to the postulates of the exchange abstraction and is supposed, among other things, to consist of an immutable substance, a substance over which time has no power, and which stands in antithetic contrast to any matter found in nature" (Sohn-Rethel, 59). In other words, coinage effects the same abuse of substance as does the commodity, the object in the shop window, itself. The exercise of coins and commodities is simply to carry abstract meaning for the purposes of exchange, and in the process their own materiality (as with the distortions of voice we see in Catherine Sloper and Verena Tarrant) is frozen and suppressed. Furthermore, we should remind ourselves of the discernible historical connection made by Sohn-Rethel between the evolution of coined money and abstractive thought in the establishment of a monetary economy in the early Greek states. It was this connection that created conditions for the "capacity of conceptual reasoning in terms of abstract universals, a capacity which established full intellectual independence from manual labour" (Sohn-Rethel, 60). Exposed vividly here are the valorized oppositions upon which capitalist economics and business practices rely. And it is this connection that describes Sloper's bourgeois temperament most accurately: the abstract vocabulary of science, geometry, and cardinal numbers (in the form of monetized value) whereby Catherine becomes available as a commodity.

There is a good argument for seeing Sloper as a "hard"-money figure—associated with the solidity of the earlier Republican values evinced by Jefferson and John Adams, who recognized the "cheat" of any discrepancy between a bank bill and the quantity of gold and silver that sanctioned it—and Townsend as belonging to the world of "soft" money, the paper world of extended credit.[13] I shall pursue some of the implications of this argument later. Here, I want to note that it is not so much the details of the debate about "soft" and "hard" money that need concern us, but rather the fact that the debate has to do with modes of material expression, with a range of questions interrogating the forms of solidity and meaning attached to a crucial order of symbolism. And that symbolism has a determinant place within the culture from which James is writing. The debate shares many of the features of his aesthetic concern to compose across his readings of Hawthorne and Balzac, readings that probe the materiality of writing itself. The fiscal battles of the 1830s–1840s and the 1870s suggest, above all, the indeterminacy of currency's symbolism and rhetoric and the inadequacy of an empiricist or directly mimetic base for evaluation and representation. These features become exacerbated by their visibility during the period of social instability, realignment of class and interest groups, and economic depression immediately prior to the excesses of the Gilded Age. Treatises such as George M. Beard's *American*

Nervousness: Its Causes and Consequences—published in New York in 1881, the year after *Washington Square*—provide physiological evidence for the damaging impact of the developing industrial practices upon mind and body and offer, as it were, an intimate material metaphor for these wider areas of instability. Irwin Unger has explained this instability in terms of specific confusions, claiming an absence of consensus on money's very definition: "Some writers held that only gold and silver coin, bank notes, and government paper that performed exchanges and passed from hand to hand functioned as money; others said bank credits and deposits also qualified. They disagreed, too, over the significance of the interest bearing debt, much of which circulated as money between interest paying periods. . . . The whole financial discussion has an air of unreality" (Unger, 36). Beard's physiological account of the effects of this "unreality" reminds us that the abstractions that so concern James in *Washington Square* are not confined to the further abstractive realm of ideas but are material events that infiltrate the very structures of feeling and behavior.

7

Prescriptions and Mirrors

The project of *Washington Square* is to explore the forms of abstraction and human paralysis detectable in the onset of corporate America during the 1830s and 1840s and in the origins of a consumer culture during the 1870s. The project takes shape in the very structure of the novel in its rare (in the Jamesian canon) specificity concerning time and place in the opening three chapters which progressively dissolves as the action of the story begins, from chapter 4 onwards. The Square itself, conceived as an "ideal of quiet and genteel retirement" from the commercial accelerations of lower Manhattan, loses its relational context within the city and comes to inhabit an area that is timeless and spaceless (*WS*, 39).[1] Both the timeless and the spaceless are defining features of the industrial production of commodities. They are equally features of the bourgeois temperament that James diagnoses in the balanced, rational discourse of Dr. Sloper and in the vacuous jangle of Mrs. Penniman's elaborate imagination. Mrs. Penniman's travesties of what is usually a prime value in James, the imaginative faculty, suggest accurately her social place, as Mary Doyle Springer has noted: "Aunt Penniman exists to reveal by her acts the real heart of darkness: that in such a milieu women ("the imperfect sex") not only cooperate passively with what the ethics of a paternalistic society makes necessary, but also cooperate actively in exploiting each other because that is what the whole system gives them to do, and gives them little else to do if they are unmarried" (Springer, 81). It is the styles of Sloper and Penniman, in company with the problematically "natural" style of Morris Townsend, that compete for the commodified Catherine, worth "eighty thousand a year" (WS, 46, 47), within the frozen world of market practice. Their competition, at a specific moment in American economic history viewed from an equally specific moment later in that history, will allow us to read a close relationship between forms of writing (the interference of romantic and novelistic procedures), forms of history, and forms of financial behavior.

We will be able to see this relationship realized in one of the main complications of the novel—Catherine's quietude. Her taciturnity and broken syntax articulate both the object of James's worry (by its paralyzed, nondialogical incapacity) and the putative alternative to it (as an increasingly impossible gesture toward authenticity and a freedom from lexical and institutional impositions). Catherine's quietude simultaneously is frozen in the material world that we experience (as a reminder of the unchangeability of commodities, their suppression of their own production) and resists such materiality (as a romantic refusal of discourse to taint itself by a world already given). James's sympathy is powerfully invested in both the inhumanity of the former and the possibilities of the latter. The simultaneity of their occasion marks a point where he may exploit the extent to which his own discourse belongs to the ideological equipment of its opposition. At the same time, this tensile arena marks also the risk James takes in the approximation between his own practice and the bourgeois temperament it seeks to diagnose. The abstractness of Jamesian design finds its uncomfortable correlative (albeit rather reductively) in the paralyzing categories of Sloper's scientism and in the sphere of exchange breached from the sphere of use to which Sloper's balancing, equalizing, nondialogical style belongs. The complex of the novel-romance comes into play again here, in James's interest in the urge, encouraged by novelistic convention, to locate the alternative worlds of fiction within the world we ordinarily experience. Such an urge is tested, for example, when

Sloper interrogates first Catherine and then Townsend on the timing of their first meeting. They are both inexplicably evasive (WS, 84, 89), and the novelistic reader is impelled to question their lie over so trivial and unthreatening a detail. And James's elisions of time and space (the two indispensable properties of the novelistic convention) are, again, features of the bourgeois mind he analyzes. For such a mind, as Alfred Sohn-Rethel notes, "time becomes unhistorical time and space ungeographical space" in order to assume a "character of absolute historical timelessness and universality" (Sohn-Rethel, 56, 49). Time, indeed, will not only be elided in *Washington Square* but will operate as a distinct temporal confusion whereby, despite its overwhelming "realistic" specificity, its chronology competes within itself for historical place to emerge as an explicitly unstable resource for finding one's bearings.

It would be a mistake to view the instability of a world rapidly being revealed as a marketplace for commodities solely in terms of the more apparent changes in the means of production. The more obvious developments in industrial technology should not conceal the effects of concomitant changes in perceptions of money itself. Gerald T. Dunne has written well on this aspect of America's shift during the early nineteenth century from an agrarian to an industrial economy:

> The rise of banking cut the fabric of tradition with an especial sharpness. . . . The growing importance of banking amounted to a revolution in the traditional system of credit, which forced profound changes in outlook and values. Sharply challenged were the old agrarian views under which gold and silver, like fields and flocks, were the true essence of wealth. Rather, wealth was changing in form to the intangible—to paper bank notes, deposit entries on bank ledgers, shares in banks, in turnpikes, in canals, and in insurance companies.[2]

Brook Thomas, in an excellent commentary on Dunne's description, has recognized the fuller abstraction and instability of what Dunne characterizes only as the "intangible" form of wealth: "In the new economy, the old theory that value was determined by the inherent properties of an object gave way to a theory that the value of an object was determined by the laws of supply and demand. Increasingly, the laws of the market, with all of its whimsical fluctuations and disregard for eternal moral truths, dictated what was valuable in American Society."[3]

Here is the paper world of confidence-men, developers, speculators, and nonmaterial value that emerged in the 1830s and 1840s and lay the ground for the second great period of industrial expansion and the beginnings of a consumer culture in the 1870s. Nowhere may the tissue of uncertainty and intangibility be seen so clearly as within a structure where economic power is measured by notes and documents, where the real and the valuable are constituted by the fabric of paper with all its inadequate and dangerous symbolism. Marc Shell notes how "paper counted for nothing as a commodity and was thus 'insensible' in the economic system of exchange"; he tells us that, in the America of the 1840s, "comparisons were made between the way a mere shadow or piece of paper becomes credited as substantial money and the way that an artistic appearance is taken for the real thing by a willing suspension of disbelief" (Shell, 15, 18). Again, paper money and writing share arenas that make similar demands upon the entrepreneur and the reader. The only form of writing produced by Dr. Sloper is the paper he leaves behind as part of his "explanation" to his patients—his "inscrutable prescription" (*WS*, 27). This form of writing clearly presents the contradiction of his office and mimes exactly the artistry of his science. It is a joke about the material appearance of writing that is meant to be taken seriously and literally.

At both the fictional and material levels, "inscrutable" writing requires further acts of recomposition to demystify its content, to make it publicly readable. The activity of forcing the signs of Sloper's writing to yield their substance, their meaning, is analogous both to the contemporary interrogation of money's substance and its expression and to the general habit of Sloper's profession, the scientific positivism of "dividing people into classes, into types" (WS, 101). Both these activities depend upon a willingness to believe in the accuracy of their modes of representation, and both specie and specimen rely on the "look" of their expressions, sanctioned by a shared valorization of mathematics.

In the case of money, particularly paper notes, we witness a dissociation of writing and its referent that literally mimes the breach of intellectual and manual labor within the industrial marketplace. The final conjunction that this equation enables is thus aesthetic. It is articulated in James's conjoined reading of Hawthorne and Balzac at the time of *Washington Square*, but it is also expressed in Emerson's *Nature*. Emerson's treatise was published in 1836, the year following the building of Sloper's house, and it is a text powerfully encoded by the transcendentalist response to America's first industrial revolution, a response to which the intellectual furniture of Henry James, Sr.'s household responded sympathetically.[4] In Emerson's chapter on language we find the question of literary and philosophical symbolism explicitly maintained through the figure of pecuniary fraud:

> A Man's power to connect his thought with its proper symbol, and so to utter it, depends upon the simplicity of his character, that is, upon his love of truth and his desire to communicate it without loss. The corruption of man is followed by the corruption of language. When simplicity of character and the sovereignty of ideas is broken up by the prevalence of secondary desires, the desire of riches, of pleasure, of power, and of praise, and duplicity and falsehood take place of simplicity and truth, the power over nature as an interpreter of the will is in a degree lost; new imagery ceases to be created, and old words are perverted to stand for things which are not; a paper currency is employed, when there is no bullion in the vaults. In due time, the fraud is manifest, and words lose all power to stimulate the understanding or the affections.[5]

Emerson's statement succinctly expresses the equation I have been suggesting throughout. The particular pertinence of *Nature* as a whole (and, indeed, of the range of Emerson's thought during the 1830s and 1840s) lies in its insistence on things being *made*, being constructed by human agency, at the very moment when such making is being disguised and beginning to be forgotten by reifying industrial practices. It is precisely this sense of its own manufacture, its own creativity, that the world is beginning to lose at the moment of *Washington Square*, and the great office of *Nature* was to remind the world of that forgetfulness. The focus of the treatise, understood historically, is to join a forgetfulness of words with a forgetfulness of reunified, genuine labor, of felt experience and the friction of the democratically human. It is a joining that achieves its figurability through fiscal deceit.

The statement I have quoted occurs in that section of Emerson's treatise that attempts to express the analogies of Swedenborgian "correspondence" in aesthetic terms: the ways in which the imagination frames and operates within the relationship between symbols and their referents. As a counter to the "rotten diction" of a corrupted language, Emerson posits the urge to "fasten words again to visible things" in order to create a "picturesque language"—a phrase in which "picturesque" (a major term in James's thinking about *The Europeans*) is intended literally as a means of effecting a "commanding certificate" of truth. Hence he argues for the materiality of the images employed in true discourse, their "emblematic" function within a system whereby "the whole of nature is a metaphor of the human mind" exhibiting how the "laws of moral nature answer to those of matter as face to face in a glass," or the "axioms of physics translate the laws of ethics" (*Nature*, 21–22). Emerson's willingness to deploy metaphors from science marks an arena shared by Sloper (and, indeed, by James himself in his thoughts on the art of fiction), but while Sloper's science denotes a propensity to privatization and dominance, Emerson's promotes fluidity and interconnectedness. It is instructive that Emerson's 1850 essay on Swedenborg is capable of using technology (from, admittedly, the preindustrial era) to maintain the sturdiness of Swedenborg's metaphysics. James never felt capable of Emerson's confidence in the "exact relation" of symbol to its substance, and he would have been deeply skeptical of the directness of the correspondence promised by Emerson's "glass." However, he remembered with affection (in reviewing James Eliot Cabot's *A Memoir of Ralph Waldo Emerson* in 1887) Emerson's reading of the "Boston Hymn," a poem that clearly suggests the exploitative economic base of the concern in *Nature* with symbols. The occasion was the meeting in the Boston Music Hall in 1863 to celebrate Lincoln's Emancipation Proclamation, which freed the southern slaves. James recalls the "immense effect" with which Emerson's "beautiful voice" pronounced the lines

> Pay ransom to the owner
> And fill the bag to the brim.
> Who is the owner? The slave is owner,
> And ever was. Pay *him*!
>
> (quoted in *Essays*, 267)

Whereas what Emerson elsewhere calls "nature's geometry" provides a decided consolation for the transcendentalist temperament, James's more acute geometry points up the crisis and instability in the alliance between science, commerce, aesthetics, and human relationships. It is in this sense of crisis that the quietude that so awkwardly expresses the commodification of Catherine Sloper has its double function: to register a resistance to the commercial world and to betoken the paralysis of genuine intercourse. It is also in this sense that we are invited to read a curious figure on behalf of James's sense of historical composition.

The figure occurs at the beginning of chapter 10 when Morris Townsend, reluctantly, visits Catherine at home following his unspoken argument with her father. He is received on Catherine's own choice of ground, a "New York drawing-room," which is given a temporal description as "furnished in the fashion of fifty years ago." What we do not know is the periodicity that is being invoked here—whether the "fifty years" is to be estimated from the point of the novel's composition in the late 1870s or from its setting in the 1830s and 1840s. It makes most sense to estimate the period from the latter point because it suggests, appropriately for Sloper's resistance to modernity, that the furnishing belongs to the preindustrial era. But by this stage in the novel we have lost our sense of the insistently specific temporality that marks its opening. Because such temporal detail is largely absent from the main action of the story, its presence here indicates the nostalgia Catherine never utters—the nostalgia that underwrites the romanticism that is the more positive aspect of her quietude. We are then presented with a closely detailed description of a particular item—the only such description in the entire novel. As Townsend begins his assertions, he glances at "the long, narrow mirror which adorned the space between the two windows, and which had at its base a little gilded bracket covered by a thin slab of white marble, supporting in its turn a backgammon board folded together in the shape of two volumes, two shining folios inscribed in letters of greenish gilt, *History of England*" (*WS*, 78). Opened up here is a play between the loosely novelistic gesture of "fifty years ago" (matching the dispersals of the novel's opening sentence), denoting, presumably, an American past, and the embellished masquerade of another past, that of England, which, within a more domestic history (in the form of Fanny Kemble's anecdote about her brother), provides the "germ" of the story. In a sense, it is a play that returns us to James's correspondence with Howells about the "items of high civilisation" listed in *Hawthorne*, a correspondence from which James proposes *Washington Square* as a determinedly "truly American" tale.

The mirror would reflect not only Townsend's self-conscious "glance" (the "gilt" in its turn rather crudely punning the guilt of his occasion) but also the surface of the *History* itself, a precious object whose only reality, concealed by its surface, is a game in which its chance and hazard are further concealed by the geometry of its rules. The description distances itself from the rhetoric of novelistic expression (measured in part, for example, by the description of Mrs. Montgomery's house at the beginning of chapter 14) and has no local function to expand our sense of character or place. It lies there in the text as an abstracted item—abstracted because of both its descriptive rarity in the novel and its contribution of absolutely nothing to the narrative. It is sheer decoration, virtually a luxury item in textual terms, and so suggests not only a version of the sphere of exchange breached from use but also a disfiguring (or embellishment) of the material simplicities of use itself. Neither is it an item of more fanciful or mysterious allegory such as we might find in Hawthorne. The mirror's surface—an important term in the Jamesian value system for its promise of otherness and alterability, dispersing the illusion of essentialist selves and objects, which also characterizes the consumer culture emerging in the 1870s by its role in the new world of social performance—is literally mimetic. It is positioned so that it reflects not the vista of the outside world beyond the two windows that frame it—a framing of an internal view by the possibilities for an external view, which thereby requestions a traditional synecdochical function for mimesis—but only an imitation text. James's self-regarding irony here incorporates the catalog of propositions about writing through which *Washington Square* negotiates its exploratory course. The mirror permits only one form of material solidity—the "gilt" letters inscribing the *History* (sustained, in both senses, by the slab of marble on its "gilded" bracket), which provide a reminder of the economic conditions enabling the building of houses in Washington Square and the writing of novels about them.

8

Dr. Sloper's Aphorisms

It has been the design of the previous chapters to outline the histories within which *Washington Square* was written. Commentators on the novel have been reluctant to respond to its historicity. Darshan Singh Maini is an exception to this reluctance in claiming, "Dr. Sloper's tragedy is, properly speaking, a tragedy of a whole way of life. It is the tragedy of the bourgeois liberal world-view at a given moment in American history." His claim, while generally suggestive, lacks the historical documentation that would render it fully expressive (the documentation, for example, that I have already urged on behalf of the novel's periodicity). The claim does, however, include an observation that provides a necessary starting point for a consideration of Sloper: "The doctor's style is primarily a question of appearances and of a sum of clevernesses. It is a syndrome of values prized by the spiritually defunct upper bourgeoisie of mid-nineteenth-century New York" (Maini, 94, 90). It is Sloper's style above all that permits access to his historical positioning.

Dr. Sloper's linguistic performance shares those features of abstraction and paralysis that we have seen are characteristic of bourgeois behavior. This sharing is seen in his predilection for aphorism, maxim, and epigram—his principal discursive tools. James already recognized, in his review of Charles Sainte-Beuve's *English Portraits* in 1875, the, in the main, "valueless" worth of the epigram (*French Writers*, 677), but Sloper's deployment of these tools goes well beyond the merely rhythmical comfort of self-satisfied generalization—it becomes a determining strategy of resistance to the process of making by bearing upon objects already prepared. As Roland Barthes has claimed of bourgeois aphorisms, "Their classical form is the maxim. Here the statement is no longer directed towards a world to be made; it must overlay one which is already made, bury the traces of this production under a self-evident appearance of eternity" (Barthes, 154–55). Such a form is entirely appropriate to the temperament Sloper exemplifies: it is not merely a matter of conservatism but of a more substantial antipathy toward change and process. It codifies and freezes the world it inhabits by isolating the objects and the people of the world from any relational context, any communal enterprise. At no point, for example, does Sloper provide Catherine with a full explanation for his disapproval of Townsend, other than to repeat his suspicion of mercenary ambition; to do so would be to invite debate and thereby incorporate a recognition of other positions. Debate includes the danger of revealing himself and his feelings more widely than he wishes, and to recognize other positions inevitably ventures the possibility that he might be obliged to change his mind. It is a vivid case of the bourgeois singularity that chooses to be blind to imaginative variousness.

Sloper's aphoristic style, then, is one that is rarely prepared to investigate process, to register possibilities for intervention by others. In the very first conversation of the novel, Sloper instructs Mrs. Penniman to "make a clever woman" of Catherine. Mrs. Penniman, a woman given to "a certain foolish indirectness and obliquity of character," attempts to respond with what she imagines to be a witty rejoinder, in tune with Sloper's manner: "Do you think it is better to be clever than to be good?" With what is to be a characteristic ploy, Sloper seizes on Mrs. Penniman's "good" and turns it to create an aphorism of his own: "Good for what? You are good for nothing unless you are clever." This has the effect of neutralizing Mrs. Penniman's position: the narrative offers it as an "assertion" (one of the more inflexible modes of rhetoric) from which she "saw no reason to dissent." Not only is the conversation sealed, its dialogical possibilities cut off, but Sloper reinvokes his aphorism the next day to display its superiority to a standard aphorism: "Of course I wish Catherine to be good. . . . She is 'as good as good bread,' as the French say; but six years hence I don't want to have to compare her to good bread-and-butter (*WS*, 33).

It is a characteristic of the aphorism, even uttered with the clever but specious versatility we see in Sloper, that it refuses to acknowledge its own form. In Sloper's case, this refusal is often expressed by his irony or by epigrammatic expression. Catherine, for all her naivete, recognizes as an "exchange of epigrams" the ironical tone whereby Sloper handles the reaches of Mrs. Penniman's imagination after Townsend's first visit to Washington Square (*WS*, 55). And Catherine, unwittingly, is forced by her pressurized prose into epigrammatic form during that dreadful evening in the library when she tells her father of her wish to see Townsend again. Against the "authority" of Sloper's "logical axiom" and "scientific truth," she can only repeat herself as her words are compelled into frozen blocks. Her moment of logical triumph, her "inspiration" as she terms it to herself, is expressed with epigrammatic balance: "If I don't marry before your death, I will not after." The stolidity of her expression is easily recognized, and its potential impact is easily defused, by Sloper's alertness to its form: "To her father, it must be admitted, this seemed only another epigram; and as obstinacy, in unaccomplished minds, does not usually select such a mode of expression, he was the more surprised at this wanton play of a fixed idea" (*WS*, 124–25). Catherine lacks the agility to play her father at his own game. What is striking here is that her choice of expression, albeit in "unaccomplished" form, measures the extent to which Sloper's aphorisms and epigrams are not only effective but also infective. Her form, precisely because it is "unaccomplished," displays overtly through its syntactical rhythm the idea of balance that underwrites its authority. Such is the subtlety of James's critique of balance that commentators of a certain liberal persuasion are inclined to read the novel as "written in a clear classical novelistic prose, an English unchanged since the time of Jane Austen, a prose in which wit and precision are simply two names for one and the same endeavour." What such a reading admires is the novel's "elegance," understood as a "deftness of epigram" and a "balance or equilibrium of tone."[1] Nothing could be further from the experience of James's fiction. We have here a misunderstanding not only of the Jamesian enterprise— which is to liberate fiction from such conventions generally and, in *Washington Square*, to recognize the paralyzing effects of balance— but also, I suspect, of Jane Austen's irony.

When Sloper avoids the explicit forms of the aphorism and the epigram, his conversations frequently tend to display their enclosed (and enclosing) nature by picking up on the single words of others to appropriate their reference for his own lexicon. This habit can be emotionally neutral, as we have seen in the discussion with Mrs. Penniman on the subject of Catherine being "good." More often, the habit is, at best, the result of a cold humor. During a later discussion in which Sloper is probing his sister on Townsend's past histories, Mrs. Penniman argues, "He would tell them to you, I am sure, if he thought you would listen to him kindly. With kindness you may do anything with him." Sloper replies, "I shall request him very kindly, then, to leave Catherine alone." The pattern is repeated when Mrs. Penniman tells him of "the most appreciative, the most charming things," Townsend has to say of Catherine and advises, "He would say them to you, if he were sure you would listen to him—gently." Sloper's response, again, picks up on her central term: "I doubt whether I can undertake it. He appears to require a great deal of gentleness." It is clear, in each case, the extent to which Sloper's lexical theft rearranges the design of the original usage. The discussion ends the chapter, and it ends with a further version of Sloper's appropriation. Mrs. Penniman tells him that Townsend "is looking for a position most earnestly," and Sloper effects his most blatant rearrangement: "Precisely. He is looking for it here—over there in the front parlor. The position of husband of a weak-minded woman with a large fortune would suit him to perfection!" (*WS*, 70–71).

More cruelly, Sloper's "cold, quiet, reasonable eye" elaborates on the fixed counters of Catherine's truncated range of broken statements.

Dr. Sloper's Aphorisms

Catherine informs her father of Townsend's proposal in chapter 11. Sloper comments upon the speed of their relationship, and when Catherine, "with some eagerness," claims that "it doesn't take long to like a person—when once you begin," Sloper instantly turns her position: "You must have begun very quickly." As Catherine pleads, "Dear father, you don't know him," Sloper again switches things to his advantage with, "Very true; I don't know him intimately. But I know him enough: I have my impression of him" (WS, 84–86). Catherine's words, in her hesitant way, are designed to invite a more engaged and expressive discourse, but the invitation is always refused; plenitude of dialogue, flexibility of positions, and full alertness toward others are not available to Sloper. Instead, he is possessed of a persuasive sinuosity, particularly when he feels threatened by opposition. He is forced by Catherine into what looks like plain statement on the question of Townsend's "mercenary" ambitions. This is one of the longest uninterrupted speeches he makes in the entire novel, delivered "slowly, deliberately, with occasional pauses and prolongations of accent, which made no great allowance for poor Catherine's suspense as to its conclusion," and that "conclusion" achieves a sinuosity that approaches aphoristic form: "If Morris Townsend has spent his own fortune in amusing himself, there is every reason to believe that he would spend yours." Catherine feels that "there was something hopeless and oppressive" in having to argue with his "neatness and nobleness of expression," and she can manage only, "His fortune—his fortune that he spent—was very small," enabling Sloper's sinuosity its final kill (again we are at the end of a chapter): "All the more reason he shouldn't have spent it" (WS, 86–87). We witness a similar pattern in the following chapter, when Sloper confronts Townsend on the same question. Townsend's stance is almost as sinuous as Sloper's—"Even admitting I attach an undue importance to Miss Sloper's fortune, would not that be in itself an assurance that I would take good care of it?"—but the older hand is easily capable of taking it further and turning it entirely: "That you should take too much care would be quite as bad as that you should take too little. Catherine might suffer as much by your economy as by your extravagance." All Townsend can do here is to break the web of words with "I think you are very unjust!"—thereby placing himself beyond the game to the point of losing his temper (WS, 91–92). Townsend's disengagement here recognizes that the more professional sinuosity practiced by Sloper is a form that polishes the glazed surface of his ideas to render impossible the necessary friction of dialogue—to offer no real context for the staccato utterances of others.

The tautological design of Sloper's rhetoric can come close to syllogism. Prior to meeting Mrs. Montgomery, for example, he anticipates his reaction to her: "If she stands up for him [Townsend] on account of the money, she will be a humbug. If she is a humbug, I shall see it. If I see it, I won't waste time with her" (WS, 94). In many ways, the dominance of Sloper's style is effected with its greatest nastiness during his interview with Mrs. Montgomery in chapter 14. It is most nasty simply because, of all the characters we meet, she is the least able to deal with it, and Sloper ruthlessly exploits her incapacity. Here, even the ironic veneer of his style is dispensed with as he relieves himself of the need for social performance in the face of someone he deems to be his inferior. His presence alone seems to inflict a state of hypnosis on Townsend's sister, and she is virtually mesmerized into acquiescing to his power. Catherine is similarly mesmerized by his "authority"; the balance of his syllogistic utterance becomes a careful strategy in his deployment of the library scene: "Have you no faith in my wisdom, in my tenderness, in my solicitude for your future?" is followed by, "Don't you suppose that I know something of men—their vices, their follies, their falsities?" (WS, 123).

These disparate statements are united by their rhythm, which gives an equality of weight to the opposition of their contents—an equality that masks the sharpness implied on behalf of Townsend in the latter. The tactic fails to work on Catherine: she retorts, "He is not vicious—he is not false!" Sloper therefore switches his tone from reasonable debate to absolutist assertion: when Catherine refuses to "believe" his judgment on Townsend, he counters with, "I don't ask you to believe it, but to take it on trust." As the text instructs us, this is an "ingenious sophism" indeed (WS, 123): when style's balance fails, the only resort is to disengage debate and substitute dogma for collaborative dialogue. At the very center of the library scene, Sloper then plays his trump card: "Of course, you can wait till I die, if you like. . . . Your engagement will have one delightful effect upon you; it will make you extremely impatient for that event." This has the force of a "logical axiom" as Catherine perceives it; here, such is the pressure upon Sloper's style, he removes even this "scientific truth" from the field of discussion: "It is beyond a question that by engaging yourself to Morris Townsend you simply wait for my death" (*WS*, 124). Sloper's sophistic strategy of removal prepares the ground for the falsity of the choice he offers Catherine at the end of the scene—to "choose" be- tween himself and Townsend. It is false because, in keeping with the bourgeois temperament, it is immobilizing. It is false because it emerges as a version of the scales that characterize that temperament—offering *either* Sloper *or* Townsend. What it prescribes are self-cancelling roles rather than the range of possibilities that underwrite genuine choice. These roles are conceived as mutually exclusive rather than interactive. All that is offered is a selection of one or the other role and adhering to it with consistency—performing the one to the exclusion of the other. Variousness and alterability are distorted here by freezing rela- tional possibilities (one of James's greatest moral lessons) into discrete functions. Sloper's rhetoric disengages any real chance of proper choosing, and its immobility, its freezing of relational variousness, is reflected in the word Sloper confiningly repeats to predict the result of his experiment: "I believe she will stick—I believe she will stick!" (*WS*, 126).

That Catherine will "stick" is to be the defining term for his expectations of her from this point onwards. It reminds us vividly of the closed world inscribed by Sloper—the world of frozen, nondialogi- cal utterance. This utterance, its principal function being to remove its objects from interactive dialogue, finds its most concentrated form in mathematics, where reference is privately and internally authorized. The phrase "abstract objectism" has been developed by V. N. Volosi- nov to describe the system of mathematical referentiality, and his account is an excellent means of identifying the "cold, quiet, reason- able eye" (*WS*, 86) of Sloper's bourgeois temperament authorized, as we have seen, by rationalist mathematics and science: "What interests the mathematically minded rationalists is not the relationship of the sign to the actual reality it reflects nor to the individual who is its originator, but the *relationship of sign to sign within a closed system* already accepted and authorized. In other words, they are interested only in the *inner logic of the system of signs itself*, taken, as in algebra, completely independently of the ideological meanings that give the signs their content."[2] The particular incapacity suggested by "abstract objectism" is given a more complex reading in the paradox noted by Theodor Adorno and Max Horkheimer, a paradox that is distinctly germane to the Jamesian exercise: "As a system of signs, language is required to resign itself to calculation in order to know nature, and must discard the claim to be like her. As image, it is required to resign itself to mirror imagery in order to be nature entire, and must discard the claim to know her" (Adorno and Horkheimer, 18).

Volosinov's account of mathematical representation aptly summarizes the closed and enclosing temperament we find in Sloper, while Adorno and Horkheimer's description of the paradox within notions of linguistic representation takes us to one of James's perennial preoccupations—his concern with the dilemma of participation and observation. This dilemma has been well summarized by Taylor Stoehr:

> The chief concern of James, throughout his career, is the possibility of full experience, and the limitations imposed upon its fullness by the conditions of experiencing anything at all. His continuing view is a pessimistic one, that the price of awareness is the loss of any advantage one might gain by it. If one enters into experience actively, one is sure to make mistakes, to miss significances, to arrive finally at full awareness only when it is too late to "do" anything except savor one's sensitivity. Alternatively, one may hold back from experience, play the part of an observer of the "drama" of life, renouncing the advantages of participation in favor of an earlier awareness of what one is missing. This latter seems to have been James's notion of the artist's choice . . . the implication being that "fullness" in experience is "awareness" rather than "participation," and that the two are mutually exclusive. (Stoehr, 124)

Both words and characters, then, may be either calculating or mimetic, participating or observant, and the competing of these positions is always troublesome for James. The dilemma is especially evident in the situation of Isabel Archer in *The Portrait of a Lady* to which James devoted a great deal of thought while writing *Washington Square*. Isabel is a character who constantly vacillates between a thirst for experience and an urge for modes of aesthetic distance that might enable experience to be known and controlled. In a sense, the dilemma presents a further working out of the competing claims of Balzac and Hawthorne, of novelistic and romantic forms—the problems of referential solidity and imaginative liberty. On the issue of language here, Stoehr again usefully summarizes James's position:

> Either there was a nameable reality independent of men and language, or there was not. If there was, it was too narrow to support the fictive imagination; if there was not, everything was fiction. Between these alternatives he found it hard to choose. So long as he could believe that his language was shared, not the private language of the extreme skeptic, he was at liberty to suppose that the reality he created might exist outside his own mind. Illusion or not, reality depended on linguistic solidarity among men. (Stoehr, 133)

The notion of this competition as presenting "alternatives" is perhaps too reductive for the continual interference of these positions in James's practice, but it is clear that he recognizes the dangers of the sealed system of referentiality he presents in Sloper's mathematical viewpoint with all its enclosed, abstract, and distancing tactics. And certainly nothing could be further from Sloper's privatizing aphorisms and epigrams than an ambition for "linguistic solidarity among men." Sloper is incapable, above all else, of any form of sharing.

Mathematics, along with the concomitant ideas of balance, rationality, and scientism, is used to authorize the bourgeois temperament because it cannot be grounded in the processes of history or society. It presents itself as an ideological apparatus that functions to deny its ideological status: that is, its refusal of material process is a means of siting itself within an arena it proclaims as practical, constructive, and above all, objective. What this objectivity denies are the very forms of process—material, social, and historical—that it seeks to suppress.

Mathematics, understood as a system of signs, is thus particularly relevant to the presentation of Sloper because it provides an extremely expressive example of his rhetorical style—nondialogical utterance. Both refuse the potency of signs and words in positions between speakers because meaning is inevitably enclosed within their respective systems. This enclosure disavows the awkwardness of any form of otherness that might threaten the balance of its stability.

It is, therefore, especially appropriate that Sloper deploys irony as the characteristic tenor of his voice. Irony is above all, claims L. C. Knights with impressive simplicity, "a form of distancing, and when it is directed toward anyone in personal intercourse its use is to prevent communication." Knights's diagnosis of Sloper's style is one of the most useful we have: "His is a mode of speech that never varies with the person or the occasion: it is dry, ironical, and wary: it is self-contained, with none of the flexibility of a genuinely responding mind. It is a form of speech designed to dominate; and in its very form— almost irrespective of what is being actually said—we can see what it is that has determined the small—that is to say the unspectacular— tragedy of Catherine Sloper." (Knights, 17). We may amplify this observation by noting that irony's "form of distancing" shares the curious liberalism of a satirist who claims to offer a critique of all positions while identifying with none. As Catherine rather wisely says somewhat later, "Men so clever as he might say anything and mean anything" (WS, 155). This special form of detachment is also a means toward complex disguise. Early in the novel we are told of Sloper, "it is a literal fact that he almost never addressed his daughter save in the ironical form." The conjunction of *fact* and *form* displays the extent to which the "ironical" is so ingrained as to become "literal" for Sloper, the real thing. The effect of his irony upon Catherine leaves us in no doubt that it is an exercise in power:

> Whenever he addressed her he gave her pleasure; but she had to cut her pleasure out of the piece, as it were. There were portions left over, light remnants and snippets of irony, which she never knew what to do with, which seemed too delicate for her own use; and yet Catherine, lamenting the limitations of her understanding, felt

that they were too valuable to waste, and had a belief that if they passed over her head they yet contributed to the general sum of human wisdom. (WS, 46)

Delicately and gently understated here is the true ugliness of Sloper's power—not starkly or nakedly a matter of force, but a confidence trick that leaves the victim with "pleasure" while being prey to manipulation. What is particularly moving is that Catherine is allowed so little sense of what is going on: Sloper's power is such that its exercise goes largely unrecognized by his daughter.

The occasion of this moment is the first conversation between Sloper and Catherine in the novel, at Mrs. Almond's party in chapter 4. And the occasion is economic. What prompts the narrative's observation on irony is Sloper's comment to Catherine: "Is it possible that this magnificent person is my child?" Her elaborate crimson gown renders her "sumptuous, opulent, expensive," a package for consumption worth "eighty thousand a year" (WS, 46). So the "literal fact" that accompanies the first appearance of the "ironical form" is immediately given solidity not only by a large amount of money but by a view of Catherine as someone who is available for exchange. The evasiveness of a tone of voice has sought specific concreteness. This interplay of fact and value emerges again during Sloper's second conversation with Townsend in chapter 12, when Townsend formally requests Sloper's approval for his engagement. Townsend argues that Catherine "seems to me quite her own mistress," and Sloper's reply registers his interference with the interstitial worlds of fact and value: "Literally, she is. But she has not emancipated herself morally quite so far, I trust, as to choose a husband without consulting me" (WS, 88). Here is another of Sloper's syntactical balancing acts. Its sophistry not only elides the worlds of fact and value for the purposes of rhetorical disguise, but it allows fact to be wholly suppressed by value in order to maintain Sloper's own authority.

The fate of Catherine, the most obvious victim of that authority, is to be effectively paralyzed by the world it represents, to be as "frozen" (to use Sohn-Rethel's material metaphor) as any object in a shop window. At the end of that crucial scene in the library in chapter 18,

Sloper's authority expresses itself through repetition, miming, as it were, its fixating capacity. As we have seen, his final word to himself (prescriptive for his entire anticipation of Catherine's future), "stick," is repeated, as is his final instruction to his daughter—"Exactly as you choose" (*WS*, 128)—even though the notion of choice, as I have suggested, is stripped of its real range of alternative possibilities. In the very next scene between Catherine and Townsend, the suitor (who shares several features with the father) effects a similar reduction of choice—"You can't please your father and me both; you must choose between us"—and sustains his reduction by responding to Catherine's fear of her father with the rationalism we associate with Sloper: "Then you don't love me—not as I love you. If you fear your father more than you love me, then your love is not what I hoped it was" (*WS*, 132–33). Sloper's physiognomy is entirely in keeping with his effect of freezing: his eyes are "cold," and the adjectives most usually applied to him all register a general physical stiffness—*firm, rigid, stiff, inflexible, indifferent, implacable*. The mere savagery of his gaze—"a look so like a surgeon's lancet" (*WS*, 128)—is insufficient and, perhaps, too assimilable as a figure for his effect. It is left to the extravagant imagination of Mrs. Penniman to go a good deal of the way toward the foolish sharpness of an oxymoron in developing a more appropriate figure. "His state of mind really freezes my blood," she writes to Townsend, and continues, "His hatred of you burns with a lurid flame—the flame that never dies" (*WS*, 173). Townsend gives his version of the figure in observing, "He combines the properties of a lump of ice and a red-hot coal" (*WS*, 174).

The effect of these conjunctions serves to dissuade us from too reductive a reading of Sloper, from seeing his capacity for freezing as merely that of cold, inhuman, insensitive tyranny. This is important because Sloper too is a victim of "unspectacular" tragedy (deliberately suppressed by the narrative beyond the brief mention of its occurrence)—the deaths of his wife and infant son. Despite his "disappointment" in Catherine, this tragedy induces a special kind of care for his daughter's future. It would be entirely wrong (particularly in a Jamesian novel) to dismiss him solely as an unyielding patriarch, and the significance of the figures presented by Mrs. Penniman and Townsend is to suggest the passion in his coldness—a human passion, born out of loss, that surpasses the enthusiasm of a scientific experimenter awaiting the result of the "mixture" he observes. This passion partly informs the excursion to Europe. We know that the excursion is conducted to take Catherine's mind off Townsend, to persuade her to Sloper's own way of thinking. But what is interesting is that the novel strategically refuses to document the excursion in any detail (*WS*, 150). Instead, it chooses to focus upon just one incident—the geographically dramatic scene in the Alps in chapter 24 where Sloper reveals his full rage. The scene has two functions. First, and most obviously, it is an appropriate setting for the freezing effect upon Catherine of his temperament. Although it is only late August, the air is "cold and sharp" and Sloper looks at her with eyes "that had kept the light of the flushing snow-summits on which they had just been fixed." The location is utterly removed from any social or relational context: it is a "high place," at "a great elevation," which to Catherine, thinking in relational terms (of Morris Townsend), seems "so desolate and lonely" (*WS*, 153). It is a "hard, melancholy dell, abandoned by the summer light," that "made her feel her loneliness" (*WS*, 154). The scene's second function is less foregrounded but very expressive of the passion we should not neglect in Sloper. It is important to see the choice of location as a romantic gesture on Sloper's part—a cathartic cry for release in recognition of the extent to which his bourgeois scientism is repressive. Here, he is not only watching his experiment develop but venting his full passionate fury. He reveals his violence for the first and only time, to the extent that Catherine not only entertains the possibility (albeit vaguely) of physical harm but speaks "in violence" herself (*WS*, 154–55).

The significance of this scene in the Alps lies, then, not so much in its occasion for visible, unprotected, and unprotecting harm as in its expression of what is otherwise suppressed by the bourgeois view of the world. Here, we recognize not only the fuller complexity of Sloper's character but the less evident effects of suppressive rigidity. These effects, again, take us out into James's wider preoccupations in *Washington Square*—preoccupations with his own art and with contemporary economics, which share the same field. It is in this sense that we need to amplify our notion of the Alps scene as nonrelational, as devoid of any mutuality beyond its own confines. Sloper, as we know, is fond of categories, and he tells Townsend in chapter 12 that he belongs to a "category from which it would be imprudent for me to select a husband for my daughter, who is a weak young woman with a large fortune" (WS, 89). While his "category" for Catherine is openly ventured (that of wealthy weakness), that for Townsend of mercenary poverty is not admitted as such by Sloper, who prefers to "say simply that you belong to the wrong category" (WS, 90). The point is that such categories are self-sealing and permit not relation but only a deterministic logic. For Sloper, nothing, not even Townsend's "word of a gentleman," will release him from the "category" Sloper has decided upon, and Sloper displays his logic in commenting, "There is nothing against you but an accident, if you will; but with my thirty years' medical practice, I have seen that accidents may have far-reaching consequences" (WS, 90). Sloper's logic, authorized by the scientific practices upon which the bourgeois imagination and progress rely, is a clear denial of relational process. By arguing that an "accident" has "consequences," he places the contingent, the onetime event, within a determinant schema of cause-and-effect that sanitizes (or balances) the potential threat of awkwardness or otherness, which might disrupt a measured world.

For James, the notion of relation (particularly between characters) is one of his greatest discoveries as a novelist. His position is stated most succinctly and most famously in his preface to *Roderick Hudson*: "Really, universally, relations stop nowhere, and the exquisite problem of the artist is eternally but to draw, by a geometry of his own, the circle within which they shall happily *appear* to do so" (*French Writers*, 1041). Sloper's logic permits not a relational understanding of people or events but only a confining pattern of cause-and-effect—the pattern that results from setting up the elements of an experiment and awaiting the result. We can see this nonrelational apprehension even in the placing of his house. Despite the fact that it "exactly resembled" the other new houses in the Square (WS, 39)—a uniformity that cannot help but suggest the image of mass-production that was beginning to characterize America's first industrial revolution—it remains merely contingent to them. There is never any sense of neighbors, or of the house belonging to any wider scheme of relationship, and its architectural uniformity serves only to stress, by contrast, its privacy. Geographically, then, the house is nonrelational; in a way, it is a nonurban domicile, and approximating itself perhaps to the social estrangement of the country house, which, elsewhere in his fiction, is James's most habitual dwelling place. One domestic anomaly is particularly striking—with a young child to bring up (and a girl at that), it is singular that Sloper never chooses to remarry despite all his obvious eligibility. We have no inkling of any female connections other than with his sisters, and Sloper recognizes how poor a substitute is Mrs. Penniman as a maternal guide. In the most intimate area of his personal life, then, Sloper chooses to be nonrelational, refuses to share himself.

Sloper's refusal to share himself belongs generally to his fixating attitude toward the world (his denial of real choice, his predilection for balance and reason, his habit of categorization), an attitude that, as I have been suggesting, is characteristic of the bourgeois mind. It extends to his treatment of Catherine: not only does he refuse to share himself, but he refuses to share his daughter. Several critics have suggested that psychoanalytical inquiry would propose this refusal as evidence of incestuous feelings (Maini, 96; Hovey, 7, 10, n. 22). This suggestion is interesting for my present argument because it can be developed on behalf of the economic history I have been claiming for *Washington Square*. Richard Godden has argued very usefully: "Incest could be read as an economic crime; the father, rather than exchange his daughter, penetrates her as he might penetrate a market, and accumulates her sexuality to his own. Incest is integrative in its denial of the mixing of different bloods and classes."[3] A resistance to exchange is a resistance to sharing, to relation. Where Sloper is concerned, more accurately, Catherine *is* available for exchange but not for use through the structure of marriage. In effect, Sloper's freezing of Catherine is to keep her (as with any object in a shop window) at the point of exchange without allowing the possibility of full transaction, of entry into the relational world. By accumulating her to himself, he repeats the function of nineteenth-century finance capital, which keeps itself inert, again, Sloper's expectation (and, indeed, wish) that Catherine will "stick" seems especially appropriate. Catherine will mirror with extraordinary accuracy the paradox of the commodity: she is there for purchase, for use, but that purchase, which would enable a relational context for her, is infinitely suspended. At the same time, the sanctity of Sloper's class position is preserved, safe within the freezing and the balance that resists the relational, the integration of other class positions, in the figure of Townsend.

9

Catherine Sloper's Quietude

Catherine herself is the object of play for the competing styles of Sloper, Townsend, and Mrs. Penniman. Her social gestures express themselves in two ways—through her clothing and her speech—and both point to her place in the shop window where commodities are displayed.

Catherine's bright, expensive dresses (the crimson gown she wears for Mrs. Almond's party in chapter 4 is exemplary) have all the consumer-orientated opulence to attract a potential purchaser. At the same time, they are distinctly at odds with her looks. She is seen by others as a "dull, plain" girl (WS, 37) whose shyness yields an impression of stolidity and insensibility (WS, 36). Her "lively taste for dress" provides her principal articulative resource: "She sought to be eloquent in her garments, and to make up for her diffidence of speech by a fine frankness of costume." But her judgment about such costume "was by no means infallible; it was liable to confusions and embarrassments," so that, "if she expressed herself in her clothes, it is certain that people were not to blame for not thinking her a witty person" (WS, 37). The overall effect is that she is "both ugly and overdressed," and although she is only twenty when she buys her "red satin gown trimmed with gold fringe," it makes her look "like a woman of thirty" (WS, 38). Even Mrs. Almond notes that "she is so large, and she dresses so richly" (WS, 61). The first conversation we see in the novel between Catherine and her father is prompted by her dress, and even the heaviness of Sloper's irony here ("You are sumptuous, opulent, expensive" [WS, 46]) cannot disguise the distance between her looks and her costume. And of course it is the *display* of the latter that counts: Sloper suggests, "You look as if you had eighty thousand a year," and when Catherine replies, "Well, so long as I haven't—," he comments, "So long as you haven't you shouldn't look as if you had" (WS, 46), cruelly underlining the breach between exchange (the appearance of value) and use (actual value) that Catherine is made to represent—the frozen condition of the commodity.

It is not, I think, fanciful to see the *front* parlor, which of all the rooms in the house, is her "particular province" (WS, 164), as the showcase for her display. The attractiveness of the house's frontage is stressed: "a handsome, modern, wide-fronted house, with a big balcony before the drawing-room windows, and a flight of marble steps ascending to a portal which was also faced with white marble." At the same time, James makes a point of insisting that the house "exactly resembled" many of its neighbors, suggesting the uniformity of industrial production and the purchase of its commodities (WS, 39). While Catherine and Sloper are abroad, Townsend, when he is not invading the doctor's study, is entertained in the *back* parlor, which is ceremonially divided off from its "more formal neighbour" by the "great mahogany sliding doors, with silver knobs and hinges" (WS, 151). The front parlor is an appropriate platform from which to exhibit one's value as worth "eighty thousand a year" (WS, 46, 47). This valuation should not be dismissed solely as an expression of Sloper's irony. It is repeated twice, and the straightforward voice of Mrs. Almond notes Catherine's "prospect of thirty thousand a year" (WS, 60). In one of the more blatant of the novel's conjunctions, we have been told already of Sloper's wife that she "had ten thousand dollars of income and the most charming eyes in the island of Manhattan" (WS, 28). The vocabulary of pecuniary acquisition infiltrates the language of all three major characters where Catherine is concerned. Both Mrs. Penniman and Townsend view her as a "prize" (*WS*, 140, 136, 142), and Mrs. Penniman's "natural disposition to embellish" (*WS*, 187) extends her "sense of the picturesque" (*WS*, 189) into a vacuous fantasy in which her heroine's triumph will be her ultimate sale. Sloper explicitly commodifies Catherine within a particularly nasty metaphor at the end of the European excursion: "I have done a mighty good thing for him [Townsend] in taking you abroad; your value is twice as great, with all the knowledge and taste that you have acquired. A year ago, you were perhaps a little limited—a little rustic; but now you have seen everything, and appreciated everything, and you will be a most entertaining companion. We have fattened the sheep for him before he kills it" (*WS*, 156–57). Even Catherine herself is not free from such vocabulary: she has a sense of breaking a "contract" with her father (*WS*, 143), and she views Townsend as "her own exclusive property" (*WS*, 164).

In a sense, the economic display of Catherine invokes a familiar theme of nineteenth-century English fiction since at the least the time of Jane Austen: the portrayal of daughters as trade-worthy and constituted for sale. If such invocation informs *Washington Square*, I want to stress that its function is not so much to denote continuity or variation within a literary tradition as to comment upon changes in history. Sloper may be conservative, but he is not old-fashioned, and it would be difficult to imagine his profession in *Pride and Prejudice* (1813), for example. The trading of the female in an Austen novel is, predominantly, a practice of social imperialism. It is occasioned, admittedly, by pecuniary considerations, but the point is that the female is there to be *used*. In 1813 exchange and use were allied, but as the market began to change with alterations in the modes of production, this alliance became disengaged. The emerging network of commodity relations in the 1830s and 1840s depended precisely on the *gap* between exchange and use. Catherine is not offered for use but for exchange only: the ghost of Austen haunts not only the choice of Austin Sloper's name but this very shift in the notion of trade as the experience of commodity begins its ascendancy. Sloper does not *need*, economically or socially, to sell Catherine, to use her: she is there for display, on behalf of revised meanings of social selling. It is a feature of his paradoxical form of resistance to the new commerce that he attempts to exploit commerce's disguising of its process of manufacture. Hence, for example, he refuses the traditional and central office of the parent to organize, or cause to be organized, a series of suitors for Catherine. And having decided upon Townsend's unsuitability, he never even tries to buy him off. Revealingly, the action of the novel begins in chapter 4 with an engagement, and there is no evidence that this is an affair of the barter we would find in Austen. Indeed, none of the marriages in the novel, slightly presented though they are, is felt to belong to trading in its older sense. Sloper's own marriage, described in chapter 1, was "for love," and the "solid dowry" accompanying his bride was virtually tangential. At the domestic level, James's choice of profession for Sloper—which eschews the historical reductiveness of the law, or Wall Street—strikingly includes an indifference toward financial resource, an indifference that is stressed at some length:

> The fact of his having married a rich woman made no difference in the line he had traced for himself, and he cultivated his profession with as definite a purpose as if he still had no other resources than his fraction of the modest patrimony which, on his father's death, he had shared with his brothers and sisters. This purpose had not been preponderantly to make money—it had been rather to learn something and to do something. To learn something interesting, and to do something useful—this was, roughly speaking, the programme he had sketched, and of which the accident of his wife having an income appeared to him in no degree to modify the validity. (*WS*, 28–29)

The sheer length of this description insists upon the size of Sloper's indifference to the hurly-burly of trade, of making money. Of course he is able to *afford* such indifference, which is made possible only by wealth in the first place. We are told that "his easy domestic situation saved him a good deal of drudgery," and that his wife's social affiliations undoubtedly gave additional value to his practice. But this value is experiential rather than financial, giving him "a good many of those patients whose symptoms are, if not more interesting in themselves than those of the lower orders, at least more consistently displayed" (*WS*, 29). By removing Sloper from those more obvious categories of profession that would provide a critical lens upon the development of bourgeois culture, James succeeds also, then, in recasting the notion of the female's trade-worthiness; a recasting that is thoroughly in line with shifts in contemporary history.

The distance of *Washington Square* from the world of Jane Austen may be seen further in James's portrayal of Catherine's style of speech. By comparison with the volubility of Mrs. Penniman, the loquaciousness of Townsend, and the sinuosity of Sloper, Catherine's style of speech—in vivid contrast to her style of dress—is virtually a negation of style. Her narrow range of expression, her silences, are given material form: she chooses a meeting with her father at eleven o'clock at night, when "the house was wrapped in silence" (*WS*, 121), and her handwriting, the most extensive use of her voice, is beautiful because of her fondness for "copying" (*WS*, 106), a fondness that reminds us of the reproducibility upon which market practice depends. Even her tears flow silently at the moments of her greatest distress: following the scene in the library with her father (*WS*, 129), and at the news of Townsend's return (*WS*, 213). Catherine's efforts to find her place between the competing claims of Sloper and Townsend lead at one point to a sensation that figures exactly the divisions and paralysis of commodity abstraction—a feeling of suspension characterizing the breach between exchange and use: "She had an entirely new feeling, which may be described as a state of expectant suspense about her own actions. She watched herself as she would have watched another person, and wondered what she would do. It was as if this other person, who was both herself and not herself, had suddenly sprung into being, inspiring her with a natural curiosity as to the performance of untested functions" (*WS*, 106).

Suspension registers the immobility into which Catherine is pressured. But here we recognize also the extent to which she herself is obliged to wield, unwittingly perhaps, the very forces that instigate her immobility. In part she is adopting a stance akin to Sloper's in watching the experiment of herself. In part she is beginning to acknowledge the need for some element of performance in her personal relations, the performance that, as we shall see, is to be a hallmark of the new social reality within consumer culture. In part she is displaying the alienation of the self that is customarily associated with the effects of developing industrialism. The occasion for Catherine's sense of suspension is her decision to try to be "a good daughter." It is a week after the scene in the library with her father, and Sloper notes how "unnaturally passive" she has become. His imagining of her at this point is structured through variations of this passivity, all of which acknowledge her negation of style, her quietude:

> He thought a little of offering to take her for a tour in Europe; but he was determined to do this only in case she should seem mutely to reproach him. He had an idea that she would display a talent for mute reproaches, and he was surprised at not finding himself exposed to these silent batteries. She said nothing, either tacitly or explicitly, and as she was never very talkative, there was now no especial eloquence in her reserve. (*WS*, 105)

Sloper's notion of muteness comes close to the effect of the notion of being "good" that Catherine is experiencing here: "The idea of a struggle with her father, of setting up her will against his own, was heavy on her soul, and it kept her quiet, as a great physical weight keeps us motionless." She is determined both that she will not surrender Townsend and that her father will not change his mind. As a consequence, "she only had an idea that if she should be very good, the situation would in some mysterious manner improve." So caught is Catherine between competing claims and conflicting emotions that she can only conceive of this goodness in its negative formations, the formations that construct the expression of her suspension: "To be good she must be patient, outwardly submissive, abstain from judging her father too harshly, and from committing any act of open defiance" (*WS*, 107). In many ways, this suspension is to be Catherine's condition throughout the remainder of the novel. As John Lucas has noted, "One notices how often the word 'rigid' is used of her in the last pages, as though she has become arrested at a certain point forever" (Lucas, 58). We notice also that, by comparison with the extravagant and expensive crimson of the dress in which we first see her, the color we associate with Catherine by the end of the novel is white—the color that is simultaneously the absence of color and the suspension of all other colors.

In the best commentary we have on the novel, Millicent Bell has written illuminatingly of Catherine's quietude, her plain words. Opposing the linguistic worlds of those who seek to appropriate Catherine, Bell argues that James "presents in the role of his heroine a style so mute and motionless as to be almost the surrender of style—a practical and intellectual 'innocence' which derives from an inability to employ any manner dictated by social or literary convention, almost, at times, a seeming inability to speak or do at all. Out of her dilemma a new style is born, a new language of authenticity" (Bell, 19). As I shall argue later, the notion of "authenticity" constructed in this way enables us to read Catherine as a figure of the 1830s and 1840s within another history—the history of changing ideas about the self during the nineteenth century. This history charts a movement for the self considered as a single, integrated being dependent upon a directness of relationship, whose actions are measured by standards of naturalness and authenticity, to the self considered as a dispersed and dispersive being dependent upon a diversity of relationship, whose actions are viewed as performances and measured by standards of social success. At present, though, I want to attend to James's obvious sympathy for that order of romanticism that valorizes quietude as a gesture toward a vanishing world of organic totality—the world of imagined harmony between humanity and labor, between humanity and nature, that is so clearly threatened by the advent of industrial practices. But while Catherine may well share romanticism's resistance to such practices, her quietude, as the product of their economic transformations, should not be seen so restrictively.

Catherine's limited speech may more expressively be considered as a version of what happens when words are disengaged from a communicative position between speakers. This nondialogical linguistic paralysis has been usefully described by V. N. Volosinov. Against the "philological type of understanding which excludes response in advance," Volosinov argues:

Any genuine kind of understanding will be active and will constitute the germ of a response. . . . To understand another person's utterance means to orient oneself with respect to it, to find the proper place for it in the corresponding context. . . . *Any true understanding is dialogic in nature*. . . . Therefore, there is no reason for saying that meaning belongs to a word as such. In essence, meaning belongs to a word in its position between speakers; that is, meaning is realized only in the process of active, responsive understanding. (Volosinov, 101–2)

Catherine certainly attempts such orientation, but Sloper permits no dialogical context to which her utterance may correspond. As the result of her father's interlocution and her own immobilized referentiality, any real understanding or response is excluded. Sloper freezes the dialogical possibilities of words just as his experimental categories freeze the relational possibilities of people. And Henry James, the great discoverer of relation as the linguistic and social organizer of fiction, the writer whose main interest is always in the ways in which his characters talk to each other, would be especially alert to the paralysis of Catherine's quietude as an issue of both language and history. The disengagement of Catherine's words from a communicative, actively dialogical position between speakers approximates, again, to the frozen condition of commodities. Her broken syntax shares the same arena as Sloper's balanced syntax: both register, in their different ways, the effects of the marketplace.

In suggesting this alternative reading of Catherine's quietude to Millicent Bell's claims for its "authenticity," I am not proposing that the latter be cancelled out. In fact I would want to argue that these two accounts be seen as complementary—and not simply because, as I shall show, such a notion of "authenticity" has a further historical resonance. James's historical sense is acute enough to recognize the need to display *both* the effects of the marketplace *and* the main putative alternative to those effects that is found in ideas of romantic organicism and harmony—the eloquent silence of nature's compacts. The point can be made through the literary models we might invoke on behalf of Catherine's quietude. The models that present themselves most readily are those of Shakespeare's Cordelia and Melville's Billy

Budd. In response to her father's request for testimonies of love, and against her sisters' hyperbolical professings, Cordelia can only speak in asides—"What shall Cordelia speak? Love, and be silent," and, "I am sure my love's more ponderous than my tongue." When forced into public statement, her muteness is maintained: "I cannot heave my heart into my mouth" (*King Lear*, I.i). Billy, too, when confronted with the loquacious and sinuous malignancy of Claggart and rendered linguistically incapable by his stammer, is pressured into physical expression: "I did not mean to kill him. Could I have used my tongue I would not have struck him. . . . I had to say something, and I could only say it with a blow."[1] The situations of Cordelia and Billy are comparable to Catherine's in that all three have to confront worlds that rely for their effects and their success on a profession of linguistic proficiency. Goneril, Regan, Claggart, and Sloper (and Townsend, to an extent) all achieve their immediate goals through the dexterity of the tongue, the dexterity that Cordelia, Billy, and Catherine are obliged, by their differing positions, to refute. Their refutation reflects the stance of Emily Dickinson's "Could mortal lip divine," a poem in which Dickinson characteristically suggests silence as a critique of expressive language. It was written around 1877, immediately prior to James's composition of *Washington Square*:

> Could mortal lip divine
> The undeveloped Freight
> Of a delivered syllable
> 'Twould crumble with the weight.[2]

Silence, constructed in these ways, clearly presents a potent resource for resistance to a material world that is largely reliant upon the manipulation of words themselves. But I want to suggest that Catherine's situation has a larger complexity. The converse of this silence is also an important Shakespearean lesson, and paradoxically, it is preached in *Washington Square* by Mrs. Penniman. The occasion is her prying into her niece's feelings following Townsend's jilting, her attempt to persuade Catherine to talk; her persuasion invokes *Macbeth*: "It will relieve you. Don't you know Shakespeare's lines?—

'The grief that does not speak!' " (WS, 190). Her allusion is to that moment in the play when Malcolm and Ross are telling Macduff of the slaughter of his family. Malcolm advises: "Give sorrow words; the grief that does not speak, / Whispers the o'er-fraught heart, and bids it break" (Macbeth, IV.iii). Mrs. Penniman may be a great abuser of words, but the Shakespearean reference has sufficient weight to alert us to the cathartic necessity for words in situations of great emotional strain. Catherine's quietude is not chosen in the way that Cordelia's, for example, is chosen. Rather, it is forced into paralysis by the linguistic world that surrounds it, a world whose style (principally that of Sloper) so accurately reflects its material base. We need to add, then, a further literary model for Catherine's quietude—Melville's Bartleby in a story subtitled "A Tale of Wall Street." Melville questions his writing practice in the context of disabled liberal-bourgeois economics, the paper arena of "rich men's bonds, or mortages, and title deeds," which is wholly separated from the world of production. That context is informed by the same principles of balance and rationalism that persuade Captain Vere's final verdict upon Billy Budd and that legitimize the profession of Dr. Sloper. Bartleby, like Catherine, is a copyist. He is a figure who habitually faces a literal wall, who resists the materiality of the world even to the extent of refusing food, whose taciturnity consists in a single phrase, awkwardly repeated ("I prefer not to"), and who ends the story in the mummifying atmosphere of a prison called "The Tombs." Thus considered, Catherine's quietude can gesture only partly to the positivity evident in the examples of Cordelia, Billy Budd, and Emily Dickinson. It registers an authenticity of resistance to an overly loquacious world but can at best be seen only as a painful reminiscence of an earlier linguistic sincerity and directness that remain as possibilities yet lack effective authority.

It is in this sense that John Lucas's phrase for Catherine's final condition, a "terrible stagnation" (Lucas, 58), is revealingly inappropriate. The phrase partakes too strongly of the organic world that she both rebuts and is rebutted by for the sake of her salability. Her condition at the end of the novel is explicitly not part of nature's process: Townsend, himself now fat and balding, tells her, "You have not changed," and notes that the years "have left no marks" (*WS*, 217). These are not merely social pleasantries. They register accurately Catherine's frozen state, her removal from nature. We can see this in another way by looking at the adjective that is most frequently applied to Catherine by the narrative—*poor*. She is described by this term on thirty-five occasions in total, but on only five occasions after being spurned by Townsend, and on none at all after her father's death.[3] Now *poor* is not a very satisfactory adjective: it creates no picture, it is amorphous and nonspecific, and it belongs to a generalizing judgment that tells us little about its subject. We use it through laziness, when we cannot be bothered, or are unable, to give a more concrete account. James is not a lazy writer, and nonspecificity of picture is among the last charges one would bring against him. His extended use of this adjective is strategic: *poor* belongs very much to the natural world of process that is increasingly refused to Catherine, and the pattern of its frequency charts her gradual progress into stasis. That stasis is so complete in its refusal of nature that, finally, the adjective can be dispensed with altogether as Catherine's condition moves her beyond even the loosest of human descriptive language. Catherine is rendered "poor" by the social world that uses her to the extent that, in the end, even such inadequate vocabulary is not available on her behalf. Her final state is thus removed from natural intercourse altogether—there is nothing more "natural" in human discourse, after all, than the lethargy of epithets such as "poor." That state is a release as well as an ultimate consequence of the bourgeois pressures she experiences in the course of the novel; so in both senses "poor" becomes unnecessary. The diminution of its frequency underlines the difficulties of human language (however insufficient) within the world of the marketplace, the world of numbers and categories that structures the monetary aspect of commodities.

So Catherine, like any commodity, is not allowed to experience material change. Comparable perhaps is Pansy Osmond in *The Portrait of a Lady*, who experiences similar unalterability by being effectively frozen into permanent girlhood by the material aestheticism of her father. Unalterability is the inevitable consequence of the abstract sphere of exchange in separation from the material sphere of use as the former begins to dominate social interaction. Alfred Sohn-Rethel makes the point well:

> The nexus of society is established by the network of exchange and by nothing else. It is my buying my coat, not my wearing it, which forms part of the social nexus, just as it is the selling, not the making of it. . . . In enforcing the separation from use, or more precisely, from the actions of use, the activities of exchange presuppose the market as a time-and-space-bound vacuum devoid of all interchange of man with nature. (Sohn-Rethel, 29)

This is the "vacuum" where Catherine ultimately rests. As we shall see, James will dissolve the temporal and geographical specificity with which the novel begins in its first three chapters, but here I want to underline the particular function of money within the network of exchange. Money operates, above all, as an equalizing factor and thus returns us to the quantitative differentiation of balance, type, and geometry whereby the opening of *Washington Square* is organized. Money itself provides an image for the abstractness of market transactions because, as Sohn-Rethel suggests, both rely upon a uniformity that elides the differences of people, locality, and date: "The uniformity finds expression in the monetary function of one of the commodities acting as the common denominator to all the others" (Sohn-Rethel, 30). The rigidity of such uniformity is the economic or mathematical equivalent to Volosinov's notion of nondialogical intercourse, and the "equality" it establishes is parallel to Barthes's "figure of the scales" as a model for the bourgeois imagination. All three rely upon a world that is perceived as ready-made and discourages difference and the grounds for human intervention. Commodities are equated in this view solely by virtue of being exchanged: transactions do not occur by any intrinsic equality the commodities may possess since there is clearly no advantage to either party in exchanging strictly equal goods or services. The "equating effect" of exchange is thus of a "non-dimensional quantity" (it is not a matter of comparing tons of cotton wool with gallons of whisky)—it is the "pure or abstract quality of cardinal numbers" that can only articulate itself by a series of relations rather than relationships ("greater than," "smaller than," "equal to"). This "non-dimensional quantity" is, then, directly comparable to the abstractions of mathematics (Sohn-Rethel, 46–47).

So Catherine Sloper is not rendered stagnant but frozen—paralyzed and removed from relationship by the pressures of the marketplace exerted through the mathematical and scientific rationalism figured in Dr. Sloper. Her fate is not the personal fate of human suffering at the hands of cruel, self-centered emotions, but that wider, historical fate of removal from humanity by the abstractions of the network of exchange. The "life" that is left her in the novel's final subordinate clause (*WS*, 220) will be devoid of life because living has been frozen by the impossibility of dialogical relationship, by the categories of the marketplace. She is sealed forever within the "parlor" that is her shop window, guaranteed now only to fade.

10

Morris Townsend's "Natural" Performances

Most commentators on *Washington Square* have, with some justice, tended to focus upon the cruelty of Dr. Sloper or the fate of Catherine Sloper. In both cases, this has led to reductive and misleading appreciations of Morris Townsend. There is no doubt that the uniformly bad press he attracts has diminished his historical resonance in the novel. A random sample suggests that the most common epithets are, of course, "fortune-hunter" and "adventurer," usually in contexts that include no substantial discussion of Townsend at all.[1] The closer analyses are more specifically condemnatory. John Lucas refers to Townsend's "coarseness" and finds him to be a "coward" (Lucas, 42, 55, 56); for F. W. Dupee, he "crudely deserts" Catherine (Dupee, 64); Mary Doyle Springer locates an "insufficiency of moral character" (Springer, 78); Stuart Hutchinson, who is generally more sympathetic toward Townsend than most of the commentators, finds that he treats Catherine "abominably" (Hutchinson, 19); J. A. Ward sees him as "a conniver and a scoundrel";[2] Robert R. Johannsen writes of his "devilish charms";[3] William Kenney regards him as "devious and calculating";[4] and Millicent Bell summarizes Townsend's character as "unnatural, unspontaneous, insincere," with a "well-developed

sense. . . . of the uses of things" (Bell, 25). It is a mistake to see Townsend merely through the type of the heartless lover or interloper. Not
only does such a view approximate to Sloper's mode of perception,
but it forces *our* reading into too unquestioning a response; we become
inhibited from realizing Townsend as a function of the social and
economic forces I have been suggesting as the novel's main preoccupation.

Several of Townsend's features match those of Sloper—match
the bourgeois temperament that sustains a view of the world as a
marketplace for commodities by a balanced, rational discourse authorized by the categories of science and the precepts of mathematics. Like
Sloper, Townsend, when under the pressure of choosing his appropriate strategy, is capable of seeing Catherine, and indeed himself, as
economic quantities. In one of his most extended meditations on the
issue of Catherine and her money, not only do we see his capacity for
economic calculation at work, but we see also a clear narrative warning
about our putative judgment of him as a fortune-hunter. Townsend,
in one of his balancing acts, is attempting to strike the "happy mean
between precipitancy and caution" after telling Mrs. Penniman of
Catherine's willingness to "burn her ships behind her":

Between the fear of losing Catherine and her possible fortune altogether, and the fear of taking her too soon and finding this possible
fortune as void of actuality as a collection of emptied bottles, it was
not comfortable for Morris Townsend to choose—a fact that should
be remembered by readers disposed to judge harshly of a young
man who may have struck them as making but an indifferently
successful use of fine natural parts. He had not forgotten that in any
event Catherine had her own ten thousand a year; he had devoted
an abundance of meditation to this circumstance. But with his fine
parts he rated himself high, and he had a perfectly definite appreciation of his value, which seemed to him inadequately represented by
the sum I have mentioned. At the same time he reminded himself
that this sum was considerable, that everything is relative, and that
if a modest income is less desirable than a large one, the complete
absence of revenue is nowhere accounted an advantage. (WS,
142–43)

Townsend *is* a fortune-hunter, but, as we are warned here, to leave him as such is to deny his effective force. After all, we see him deliberately turning down a marriage that would guarantee him "ten thousand a year." It is at this point also that Townsend mimes Sloper's other principal model of figuring situations in mathematical terms: "Doctor Sloper's opposition was the unknown quantity in the problem he had to work out. The natural way to work it out was by marrying Catherine; but in mathematics there are many short cuts, and Morris was not without a hope that he should yet discover one" (*WS*, 143). In fact this model is to structure Townsend's entire sense of Sloper's attitude—as he says after Sloper's return from Europe, "He will never give us a penny: I regard that as mathematically proved" (*WS*, 174).

Sloper's tone is particularly apparent in the patronizing irony of Townsend's voice during his second secret meeting with Mrs. Penniman (*WS*, 138–41), and she is later, predictably, to acclaim the "charm" of what she recognizes as his "formula" for surrendering Catherine (*WS*, 176). Townsend's final letter to Catherine, explaining this decision, scientifically computes them both as "innocent but philosophic victims of a great social law" (*WS*, 196). Earlier, having "curtly" wished that Catherine would "hold fast" to her relationship with himself (*WS*, 113), he rapidly appropriates Sloper's term *stick* (*WS*, 135, 139), a term that, foremost in Sloper's lexicon of his daughter, points up exactly the paralyzed world maintained by both science and business practice.

Townsend's approximation to the abstractive and paralyzing sensibility of Sloper is, however, only part of his force in the novel. He is given the first item of direct speech as the action of the narrative begins in chapter 4: "What a delightful party! What a charming house! What an interesting family! What a pretty girl your cousin is!" (*WS*, 43). Townsend can resort to staccato speech, particularly in responding to the imposition of Sloper's sinuosity—in replying to Sloper's charge of "mercenary," for example (*WS*, 91)—but here, rushed together, are the discrete units for the more expanded discourse of polite conversation. The speech has a tendency toward the nondialogical tenor of Sloper's style. Catherine is rendered mute (albeit not uncomfortably so): "She answered nothing; she only listened," and "she felt tongue-tied" (*WS*, 43). But Townsend's style is clearly less dominating than Sloper's at this point. The difference is that Townsend's condensed utterance (with its implicit reluctance to grant discursive leeway) marks his distance from, and perhaps his awkwardness within, the social occasion. The observations he makes are, we are told, "of no great profundity," but from Catherine's stance it is his delivery that is impressive; that delivery elides the staccato structure of his syntax as he goes on "to say many other things in the same comfortable and natural manner" (*WS*, 43). Her own social awkwardness leads her to see this "manner" as oddly paradoxical: "Catherine had never heard any one—especially any young man—talk just like that. It was the way a young man might talk in a novel; or, better still, in a play, on the stage, close before the foot-lights; looking at the audience, and with every one looking at him, so that you wondered at his presence of mind. And yet Mr. Townsend was not like an actor; he seemed so sincere, so natural" (*WS*, 44).

Catherine's mixture of the theatrical and the natural bespeaks, first of all, that particular difficulty of apprehending the unexpected, the new, from a position of entrenched stability. Her conjunction of these antithetical discourses displays her uncertainty—the uncertainty that stems from the problem of finding an appropriate social vocabulary for forms of otherness. Something similar happens in *The Europeans*. Again, the occasion is a first meeting—here, between Felix Younger, one of the Europeans of the novel's title, and his cousin Gertrude Wentworth, the indigenous channel through which the limitations and the possibilities of the New England temperament of the 1840s are expressed. Gertrude is reading a volume from the *Arabian Nights*, and Felix appears as if from one of its stories: "There, for a quarter of an hour, she read the history of the loves of Prince Camaralzaman and the Princess Badoura. At last, looking up, she beheld, as it seemed to her, the Prince Camaralzaman standing before her. A beaut' ful young man was making her a very low bow—a magnificent b such as she had never seen before. He appeared to have dro from the clouds."[5] This is clearly a more highly colored mome Catherine's first sight of Townsend, but it does provide son parallels. Gertrude is not left mute, but the "surprise" of the newness she experiences keeps her "sitting still"—"She had never in her life spoken to a foreigner" (*Europeans*, 53). Felix's newness (and that of his sister, Eugenia) is to be profoundly disturbing for the New Englanders. It is expressed through the diffusive, nonspecific terms they have difficulty in comprehending: Felix is "foreign," "European," "bohemian," and "amateur," a man of no definable place or profession. The only language available to the New Englanders for articulating this newness is that of fantastical romance, a language that attempts to accommodate the otherness they see in Felix and Eugenia by foregrounding the exoticism of the brother and sister—an exoticism that can partially approach the meaning of the new. So a few pages later, Gertrude's response to Eugenia is to see her as "the Queen of Sheba" (*Europeans*, 56), while Mrs. Acton, the novel's ailing Emersonian matriarch, has an impression of "a lady whose costume and manner recalled to her imagination . . . all that she had ever read of the most stirring historical periods" (*Europeans*, 165).

The New Englanders' romantic resource is a precursor to Catherine's theatrical resource, and it serves to remind us of James's accompanying preoccupation with the shapes of his own art, shapes that in their turn belong to the social history he narrates in both novels. The illuminating recognition here is Gertrude Wentworth's idea of artists: "They seemed to her a romantic and mysterious class, whose life was made up of those agreeable accidents that never happened to other persons" (*Europeans*, 87). The key word is *accidents*. Its awkwardness is defused by being "agreeable," but nevertheless it purposively opposes the "well-ordered" consciousness of New England exemplified in Mr. Wentworth (*Europeans*, 71), which anticipates the balanced, scientific rationalism of Dr. Sloper. Wentworth is thus prone to the muteness experienced by Catherine Sloper and Gertrude Wentworth at the interruption of newness, feeling "paralysed and bewildered" by Eugenia's "foreignness" (*Europeans*, 86) and the world of "accidents" r social artistry threatens. It is in these terms that the initial impact hat interruption is expressed: "What seemed paramount in this t enlargement of Mr. Wentworth's sympathies and those of his rs was an extension of the field of possible mistakes; and the doctrine, as it may almost be called, of the oppressive gravity of mistakes was one of the most cherished traditions of the Wentworth family" (*Europeans*, 72).

The world of "accidents" and "mistakes" belongs to the universe of chance, hazard, and speculation—to all that resists the "well-ordered" logic of cause and effect; we remember that within the categorizing habits of Dr. Sloper, "accidents" have "consequences" (*WS*, 90). For the New England temperament, "accidents" are uncomfortable because they involve multiplicity, and hence hazard, as opposed to singleness, and hence stability. It is significant that, finally, Gertrude is the only member of the New England community to reveal herself as capable of imaginative flexibility—or, indeed, of any imagination at all—and that it is this very capacity that is seen by her sister Charlotte as "dangerous and irresponsible." Again, for Charlotte this imparts a sense of the strangeness of newness: "to make her sister a strange person who should come in suddenly, as from a journey." By comparison, Charlotte's own capacity is rendered carefully stable by its domestication: "Charlotte's imagination took no journeys whatever; she kept it, as it were, in her pocket, with the other furniture of this receptacle—a thimble, a little box of peppermint, and a morsel of court-plaster" (*Europeans*, 75–76). Her hope is that the hazard of abroad will be neutralized by the safety of home. It is not insignificant that one of Morris Townsend's most sustaining features is that he is an extensive and inveterate traveler. At the aesthetic level, this opposition returns us to James's negotiation of the Hawthornesque romance. Part of the anticipated project of *The Europeans*, as James outlined it in a letter to William Dean Howells of March 1877, was to "play havoc" with the New England background in the novel (*Letters II*, 106). His sense of "havoc" is closely allied to the "latitude" he admires in Hawthorne's work for its imaginative liberty and capacity for variousness, and in many ways the interruption by the newness and otherness of Eugenia and Felix within the "well-ordered consciousness" of the Wentworths can be read as a recapitulation of the roles of Hester Prynne and, above all, her daughter Pearl in Hawthorne's *The Scarlet Letter* (1850), in which imaginative flexibility finds its foe in the singleness of Puritan symbolism. At the social level, Morris Townsend clearly belongs to the newness that may be expressed through chance and speculation.

Townsend himself picks up Catherine's confused conjoining of the theatrical and the natural a little after their initial meeting. This occurs during the first conversation he has alone with Catherine in Washington Square, and revealingly, it is offered in the context of one of the most important Jamesian tenets—the liberty of individual perception: "He had been to places that people had written books about, and they were not a bit like the descriptions. To see for yourself—that was the great thing; he always tried to see for himself. He had seen all the principal actors—he had been to all the best theatres in London and Paris. But the actors were always like the authors—they always exaggerated. He liked everything to be natural" (*WS*, 57). His smile has just made Catherine think of "a young knight in a poem" (*WS*, 56). It is Felix Younger's smile that strikes Charlotte Wentworth at his first appearance, and it is, in part, a tactic: "He smiled—smiled as if he were smiling on purpose" (*Europeans*, 52). The repetition here underlines the performativeness. Catherine observes of Townsend, "His talk, however, was not particularly knightly"; it is "light and easy and friendly; it took a practical turn" (*WS*, 56). In other words, Townsend's smile, too, is performative: the naturalness he is to proclaim within the next page of the novel is implicitly recognized as a main feature of his social artifice.

Sloper is shortly to make a joke about this very topic. When Mrs. Almond reiterates the lesson of perceptual freedom in arguing that "the thing is for Catherine to see it" ("it" being Sloper's case for Townsend as a "plausible coxcomb"), he replies: "I will present her with a pair of spectacles!" (*WS*, 65–66). The abstractions of the novel are such that naturalness itself becomes enlisted on behalf of a determinant artifice. John Lucas, in disagreeing with Richard Poirier's reading of *Washington Square* as a variation on "a melodramatic fairy-tale," points us in the right direction when he notes: "If the characters *do* become like stock types in stage melodrama and fairy tale . . . it is because they see themselves called on to play parts created by their self-conscious awareness of what their society requires of them" (Lucas, 39; cf. Poirier, 166). I do not share Lucas's faith in the characters' "self-conscious" awareness of social imperatives; as I shall show later, the notion of social performativeness is a good deal more complex than he seems to recognize. Nevertheless, Lucas's argument does suggest the linguistic disablement of social conditions, the conditions of accelerated industrial and commercial enterprise that impose the abstract structure of commodity exchange upon human relationships. Catherine is unable to figure Townsend's conversation in any but theatrical terms because it is so unfamiliar to her and she had no other terms available to her. She acknowledges an artifice so unreal—by comparison with, say, that of Mrs. Penniman—that it seems a form of the natural. Mrs. Penniman, the most explicitly theatrically inclined character in the novel, marks the extreme disablement of such language: as an unmarried woman, she is obliged to have no function other than to cooperate within the social nexus by means of her melodramatic machinations.[6] Sloper displays his degree of control over the idea when he informs Townsend, "I am not a father in an old-fashioned novel" (*WS*, 93).

If any single word dominates *Washington Square*, it is *natural*, or its variants. And substantially by far the largest number of its occasions refer to Townsend. It provides the theme for his first open tribute to Catherine: " 'That's what I like you for; you are so natural. Excuse me,' he added; 'you see I am natural myself' " (*WS*, 57). His sense of his "fine natural parts" (*WS*, 142), combined with a confidence of manner, forms the basis of his physical attractiveness, to which not only Catherine and Mrs. Penniman but even Sloper respond. Despite the fact that his naturalness constitutes a large part of his social artifice, there remains an important sense in which it may be read in terms that properly reflect its common usage. I have been suggesting that to dismiss Townsend as a social climber or a fortune-hunter serves only to fix him too unproblematically. What is insisted upon throughout is his sense of being out of place: he feels "a great stranger in New York. It was his native place; but he had not been there for many years. He had been knocking about the world, and living in queer corners" (*WS*, 44). Catherine's early impression, coupled with her theatrical metaphors, is that "he's more like a foreigner" (*WS*, 51). His main feature is mobility. He has traveled extensively abroad prior to the commencement of the story, and he returns to his travels after his failure with Catherine. Townsend's mobility is matched by his social indeterminacy. We know little of his family history, save his connection with Mrs. Almond's family, his sister, Mrs. Montgomery, who lives in reduced circumstances; we know that he has been "wild" in his youth (a notoriously nonspecific term), and that his branch of the Townsends is not "of the reigning line" (*WS*, 59). The interstitial social area in which James locates Townsend is, of course, characteristic of a period of intense development and change whereby existing class lines became blurred and the great effort of someone in Townsend's situation was to move beyond them, to articulate some proper shape. The problem for the historically alert artist (as E. M. Forster was to encounter with Leonard Bast in *Howards End* [1910], D. H. Lawrence with Paul Morel in *Sons and Lovers* [1913], and, to a lesser extent, Theodore Dreiser with Clyde Griffiths in *An American Tragedy* [1925] during a later period of accelerated transformations) is to render this mobility of social place. How is such newness to be described in the world, this new style that is invariably at odds with existing social styles?

In refusing Townsend either place or profession, James recognizes his social newness, his unavailability for the customary hierarchical definitions of societal identity. Even Sloper's taxonomical eye, supported by 30 years of experience, can do little more than locate Townsend, rather vaguely, in the wrong category (*WS*, 90). Sloper, and the world he exemplifies, has enormous difficulties in finding a category for that which has no category: his scientism, for all its justification through experiment, lacks the flexibility (and, indeed, willingness) to acknowledge the indeterminate and the new.

It is striking that within a few years James was to publish the only two novels in which he would attempt full-blown literary realism. These are *The Princess Casamassima* and *The Bostonians*, both published in 1886, and in each the central characters, Hyacinth Robinson and Verena Tarrant, are figures who belong to a similar social indeterminacy. In *The Bostonians* Olive Chancellor tries to account for the effect Verena's newness has upon her, and she is obliged to resort to the romanticist approximations we have noticed in Catherine's first impression of Townsend and in Gertrude Wentworth's initial encounter with Felix Younger:

> She was so strange, so different from the girls one usually met, seemed to belong to some queer gipsy-land or transcendental Bohemia. With her bright, vulgar clothes, her salient appearance, she might have been a rope-dancer or a fortune-teller; and this had the immense merit, for Olive, that it appeared to make her belong to the "people," threw her into the social dusk of that mysterious democracy which Miss Chancellor held that the fortunate classes know so little about, and with which (in a future possibly very near) they will have to count.[7]

Olive's account may be inflated and romantic, in terms of its obvious social wish fulfillment, but it captures again the reliance on the theatrical as a means of accommodating newness, and her romance of the "people"—"the social dusk of that mysterious democracy"—does picture the flux from which characters such as Verena, Hyacinth, and Townsend take their indefinable shape. All three are caught at a moment of change, and for existing and established social mores, the effects of this change are nowhere more confusingly presented than in the matters of place and profession.

When she is told that Townsend has no "business," Catherine expresses the surprise of one who "had never heard of a young man—of the upper class—in this situation" (*WS*, 52). Townsend, of course, does not belong to the "upper class": James's partial parenthesis here indicates the extent to which Catherine is unable to view societal organization much beyond her immediate, carefully circumscribed circle. At the same time, her assumption, however naively held, does suggest a degree of success in Townsend's manipulation of his performances. At the top of Sloper's list of inquiries about Townsend is "What is his profession?" (*WS*, 59). In the work of a writer who rarely subjects a character to a "profession" in its full material sense, we are especially alert to this insistence in *Washington Square*. It is, after all, a novel that begins with a highly complex diagnosis of "profession"—the profession of Dr. Sloper, which invokes the social and economic conditions of the history that is realized through the text. James's

Hawthorne, so fertile a preparation for the novel's concerns, makes a famous statement on the subject:

> It is not too much to say that even to the present day it is a considerable discomfort in the United States not to be "in business." The young man who attempts to launch himself in a career that does not belong to the so-called practical order; the young man who has not, in a word, an office in the business-quarter of the town, with his name painted on the door, has but a limited place in the social system, finds no particular bough to perch on. (*Hawthorne*, 45)

The writing profession and its social reception are James's principal concerns here, but his stress on the necessity for being "in business" extends beyond the fragile status of creative writing. It is the distinguishing feature of Townsend's condition that, in the social and commercial world of lower Manhattan, he "finds no particular bough to perch on." His failure to have a "career" is, then, a prime cipher of the mobility and indeterminacy that circumscribe his "naturalness" as a tactic against the styles of Washington Square. Townsend's position is "natural" in the sense that there exists no societal vocabulary whereby it may be given expression; it has no "name" in the public realm, no door on which it can be painted for recognition.

Townsend claims, eventually, to have acquired a career. We have to be doubtful about his veracity on the subject—his evasiveness suggests that he may well be lying—but, nevertheless, it is a career that is particularly germane to the period in which the novel is set. During the textual hiatus of Catherine's trip to Europe, when we see little of him other than his invasions of Sloper's study, he gains a partnership with a "commission merchant." Whether or not Townsend is telling the truth, the "particular bough" he claims is given a place—Duane Street—and although his "name" may or may not be "painted on the door," he is possessed of "little printed cards" that manage to impress Mrs. Penniman (*WS*, 160). His function is to mediate between manufacturers and the selling of their products, particularly in foreign markets. As such, according to Norman Sidney Buck, the commission merchant was probably "the most important figure in the foreign trade organization of both the United States and Great Britain." This was particularly true of the state of New York, for which the census of 1840 listed 1,044 commission houses, as contrasted with 469 commercial houses.[8]

What is illuminating about this choice of profession for Townsend goes beyond its specific historical typicality. It incorporates that form of agency that is disengaged simultaneously from the systems of production and the immediate systems of selling. In other words, it exposes a most apposite figure for the disengagement and abstraction that characterize a period of rapid industrial development—the very features that in turn provide the focus for James's critique of bourgeois economy, based on his sense of how they infect the structures of feeling constituting the liberty of human relationships. The world of Townsend's eventual profession is, then, a paper world, shared with his cousin Arthur, the "stout young stockbroker" who is the brief spokesman for the city's transformations (*WS*, 50) and the novel's only other businessman. It is a world that is wholly devoid of material process or any real contact with productivity. As paper, it is reminiscent of the alarming instability of that final abstraction, money itself, which, as we have seen, dominated American political thought during the periods of the novel's action and its composition. The location of Townsend's supposed office is in "a place peculiarly and unnaturally difficult to find." This is the excuse he gives to Mrs. Penniman for not allowing an "interview" there following the return of Catherine and her father from Europe. We may, however, take his excuse literally as a general image for the undecidability not only of the location itself but of the truth of Townsend's career. This undecidability is then underlined further by the fact that the interview eventually does take place "during the hours at which business might have been supposed to be liveliest," and that it occurs in an equally vague place, "a street corner, in a region of empty lots and undeveloped pavements" (*WS*, 174). Places and profession mirror each other here: both locations mime exactly the shadowy nature of the job and, more widely, Townsend's membership in a new, emerging, changing class that, as yet—again—has no name.

The shadows we note here should be joined to those I addressed earlier—the vagueness of Townsend's familial history and the general difficulties of finding an adequate social vocabulary for him. They belong also to a particular worry James has about characterization. In his portrayal of Townsend, James is making a further point about the presentation of character: he is realigning an imbalance he notes in Hawthorne's presentation of Holgrave in *The House of the Seven Gables*, an imbalance he remarked upon shortly before beginning to write *Washington Square*. James saw Holgrave as "a kind of national type," a "type" that foreshadows a way of looking at the aspect of Townsend that is possessed of "fine, natural parts": "Holgrave, the modern young man, who has been a Jack-of-all-trades . . . is an attempt to render a kind of national type—that of the young citizen of the United States whose fortune is simply in his lively intelligence, and who stands naked, as it were, unbiased and unencumbered alike, in the centre of the far-stretching level of American life." This is certainly a more sympathetic version of the figure Townsend is, but the main features are surely shared by both—a "Jack-of-all-trades" (an alternative image to Townsend's itinerancy) whose naturalness is seen as an absence of style, and who is "naked," "unbiased," and "unencumbered." Holgrave's modernity is glossed by his "lack of traditions, his democratic stamp, his condensed experience," and expressed in these terms, his opposition to Judge Pyncheon again throws a light on the relationship between Townsend and Sloper. The portrait of Pyncheon is, for James, "the portrait of a superb, full-blown hypocrite, a large-based, full-nurtured Pharisee, bland, urbane, impressive, diffusing about him a "sultry" warmth of benevolence, as the author calls it again and again, and basking in the noontide of prosperity and the consideration of society; but in reality hard, gross, and ignoble." What worries James is the imbalance of the portraiture here: "It is perhaps a pity that Hawthorne should not have proposed to himself to give the old Pyncheon-qualities some embodiment which would help them to balance more fairly with the elastic properties of the young daguerreotypist—should not have painted a lusty conservative to match his strenuous radical." The result is that "the mustiness and mouldiness of the tenants of the House of the Seven Gables crumble away rather too easily." James was prompted by this reading to note again the politics of Hawthorne's historical sense: Hawthorne is seen as "an American of Americans" through his "mistrust of old houses, old institutions, long lines of descent" (*Hawthorne*, 122–124).

Dr. Sloper may not be "old" in this sense, and his house in Washington Square certainly does not "crumble away," but he is clearly perceived as part of an earlier order that the "modern" Townsend seeks to challenge. In *Washington Square* James corrects the imbalance of portraiture he finds in *The House of the Seven Gables* by granting a larger potency to the Pyncheon-Sloper figure. And in Townsend he attempts a further correction to what he sees as a limitation in the presentation of Holgrave, who "is not sharply enough characterised; he lacks features; he is not an individual, but a type," and who, tellingly for the nexus of Hawthorne-Balzac with which I began, "is one of the few figures, among those which Hawthorne created, with regard to which the absence of the realistic mode of treatment is felt as a loss" (*Hawthorne*, 124). Such absence of presentation is, in the writerly sense, another shadow, here to be fleshed out by shadowiness in its societal form—Townsend's uncertain shape within the accelerations of the 1830s and 1840s. James's further advance on Hawthorne is to see the clash between old and new as not simply a matter of the demise of the one faced by the triumph of the other. In any case, even while I argue for a larger sympathy for Townsend, it would be wrong to attach to him the moral positivity both Hawthorne and James find in Holgrave. More accurately, James employs the formula of old-new to recognize the structures of transition between the two and the shadowiness of that process for literary expression. Crucially, he understands that the new incorporates not so much the death of the old as a reworking of the path followed by the old. Sloper's physical death marks not the demise of his world but the continuation of its rationality, the rationality that organizes his final illness. Catherine receives very careful instructions: Sloper "told her which of his fellow-physicians to send for, and gave her a multitude of minute directions." The last spoken words we hear from him express all the regimentation of a lifetime's science: "I shall need very good nursing. It will make no difference, for I shall not recover; but I wish everything to be done, to the smallest detail, as if I should. I hate an ill-conducted sick-room, and you will be so good as to nurse me on the hypothesis that I shall get well." The narrative itself underscores his rigidity here: "He had never been wrong in his life, and he was not wrong now" (*WS*, 207). With equal chill, his last written words, the codicil that reduces his bequest to Catherine, also perpetuate the regime that has dominated the novel.

It is James's reworking of Hawthorne's account of the clash between old and new that allows Townsend his most urgent historical presence. To read Townsend merely as a social climber is to do no more than incorporate the partiality of Sloper's own typology. Townsend presents a threat, certainly, but its real danger is that it cannot be fully formulated. This is partly because of his uncertain social positioning, but also because of a specific aspect of Sloper's bourgeois temperament. As Ronald Barthes has argued, it is a feature of the bourgeois mind— and, I would add, of the exchange relation that characterizes the disposal of commodities, the defining objects of the bourgeois universe—that it obscures "the ceaseless making of the world" (Barthes, 155). What Townsend's mobility and his interstitial placing threaten above all is exactly an exposure of the "making" of the world *via* his putative progress through it. To resist (to paralyze) Townsend is, in effect, to erase the "making" of Sloper's own location because the bourgeois idea of itself is, in Barthes's definition, of "the social class which does not want to be named" (Barthes, 138). The potential interruption of Townsend marks precisely the path Sloper himself has followed within the social hierarchies of lower Manhattan. James jotted down the "germ" of *Washington Square*, Fanny Kemble's story of her selfish and impecunious brother, in a notebook entry dated 21 February 1879 (*Notebooks*, 11–12). A few weeks earlier, in an entry dated 12 December 1878, he had sketched out an idea for the story that he completed on 17 January 1879, "The Diary of a Man of Fifty." This latter idea presents a much kindlier version of Townsend's recapitulation of Sloper, of the relation between the new and old. The entry stresses the strength of the idea for James at the time of the novel: "It has often occurred to me that the following would be an interesting situation.—A man of a certain age (say 48) who has lived and thought, sees a certain situation of his own youth reproduced before his eyes and hesitates between his curiosity to see at what issue it arrives in this particular case and the prompting to interfere, in the light of his own experience, for the benefit of the actors" (*Notebooks*, 8).

Beyond the general shape of the idea, comparison with the situation of Sloper and Townsend ceases to be illuminating: "curiosity" is a much paler, more humane emotion than Sloper's experimentalism, and his "interference" for the benefit of others is the last thing he would intend, particularly given his urge to suppress Townsend. That suppression is impelled by the danger he recognizes in Townsend as a societal creature. What Townsend most profoundly threatens is nothing so crude as Sloper's own position, or even the financial spoliation of his daughter, but the revelation of process, of "making"—of alterability, of moving beyond the confines of his classification. It is only through such alterability that the world is properly revealed as manufactured, as precisely not the ready-made entity that is the dream of the bourgeois imagination. Townsend's fluidity, his version of naturalness, proposes to dissolve the geometry by which Sloper and the Square are maintained paradoxically against the "mighty uproar" of trade and the "base uses of commerce" (*WS*, 39)—those disturbances that themselves find their enabling conditions in the abstractions of science and mathematics. Sloper's treatment of Townsend is exemplary of the conservative resistance to the new, of the bourgeois disguising (or deliberate blinding) of itself. Townsend becomes the novel's less obvious victim—the victim of the period's transformations as he struggles within its simultaneous promise of economic amelioration and damnation of those whom its accelerations leave behind.

11

Shapes of the Self—I: Manners

Literary texts can never contain their prevailing preoccupations within their own confines. The dust jacket that encloses each text as a distinct and separate object in the bookcase is only a temporary or provisory sign of completion. The occasion of *Washington Square*—the concerns with a specific history and with the concomitant presentations of self and of character—inevitably spreads itself more widely within the texts immediately adjacent to it. In particular, these are *The Europeans*, published two years earlier, and *The Portrait of a Lady*, published a year later. The history I have been charting so far has been predominantly a history of economics. I want to readjust the focus and reconsider that history in terms of its further reconstructions of the self. These reconstructions are to be seen through the changing shapes of manners—of the means whereby people conducted their intercourse in the social and commercial spheres at a time when such intercourse was being radically reorganized by the habits encouraged by consumption. This history of manners, in substantial part, has been brilliantly documented recently by Karen Halttunen, and the story she tells is indispensable for illuminating the performativeness we have noted in Morris Townsend (which is more elaborately explored through

James's characterizations of Eugenia Munster in *The Europeans* and Serena Merle in *The Portrait of a Lady*) and James's use of the 1840s from the viewpoint of the 1870s.

Drawing her evidence from fashion magazines, from advice literature on etiquette and the rituals of mourning, and from domestic ceremonies such as parlor theatricals, Halttunen, proposing that the break occurred during the 1850s, graphs the shift from what she terms "sentiment"—candor, openness, the cult of sincerity—as the presiding feature of manners to theatricality as a necessary social maneuver:

> By the 1850s and 1860s, the American middle classes were learning to distinguish between an evangelical Christian trust based on heartfelt sincerity, and bourgeois social confidence based on proper social forms; and they were deciding to rely upon the latter. They were learning to place confidence not in the sincere countenance but in the social mask; to trust not in simple dress but in elaborate disguise. Finally, they could rest secure in the knowledge that heart cannot meet heart in a world of strangers, and in the recognition that the uncloaked heart is the most dangerous acquaintance of all.[1]

The danger of the "uncloaked heart" lies precisely in its singleness of angle, expressed through candor and sincerity, within a world that is increasingly reliant on multiplicity, on performance, for its procedures. As the *Bazar Book of Decorum* warned in 1870, "If every one acted according to his heart, the world would soon be turned upside-down" (quoted in Halttunen, 167). An increasing attention to fashion and cosmetics, literal mechanisms for altering the self, from the 1850s onwards resulted in "dress as a form of disguise" whereby "middle-class women were clearly leaving behind the sentimental insistence on the candid countenance" (Halttunen, 163), and "sentimental anxieties about the hypocrisy of social disguise and formal ritual were yielding before a growing middle-class fascination with the theatrical arts of everyday life" (Halttunen, 174). This movement from the sentimental demand for transparent sincerity to the more worldly demand for skillful social performances (Halttunen, 189) matches a movement in the nature of goods themselves in the marketplace. Halttunen's analysis does not extend to this connection, but it seems clear to me that the performative aspect of manners closely approximates the way in which goods are marketable mainly for their exchange value. Objects become salable not so much for their supposedly intrinsic virtues or functions, but for their display of properties, their social resonances, in short, for their effects—the effect, for example, of a crimson dress that announces a value of "eighty thousand a year" (WS, 46).

The cult of sincerity flourished "in its purest form" (Halttunen, 189) between 1830 and 1850, the period James chose as setting for both *Washington Square* and *The Europeans*. Its slippage into performance and the world of surface, characteristic of the 1870s when both novels were written, was not simply a matter of displacement: a large part of the sophistication (and the importance) of James's historical sense is that it is always prepared to recognize the *processes* of change rather than merely its visible symptoms. In *The Europeans* it is the character of Felix Younger that traces this slippage by marking the moment when candor and sincerity are obliged to construct types, manufactured faces of themselves. It is Felix who mediates between the trustfulness and sincerity of the indigenous New England of the 1840s (in the form of the Wentworth family, his American cousins) and the achieved, burnished surface and performance that characterize the manners of the 1870s (in the form of his sister, Eugenia Munster). It is Felix who locates the anxiety of post-Jacksonian America as the country experienced the accelerated industry and commerce witnessed by *Washington Square*, the anxiety of an intensely mobile culture whose inhabitants (Morris Townsend is exemplary) sensed a placelessness in an open society where they were continually moving among strangers and confronting the problems of face-to-face contact—the difficulties of "sincere" social intercourse in a world increasingly structured by the variousness (and hence, here, the deceits and hypocrisies) necessary to the marketplace and the new commercial forms. This anxiety expressed itself on the issue of sincerity by, paradoxically, cultivating appropriate or effective shapes for the display of candor, shapes that in turn animated subsequent performativeness. As Halttunen puts it:

> Ironically, the many social laws and rituals that went into the skilled performance of middle-class gentility after mid-century had origi-

nated in sentimental anxieties about theatricality in face-to-face social conduct. To escape the hypocrisy of fashionable forms and rituals, sentimentalists expressed a belief in sentimental typology, which stated that all forms of dress and conduct should be the outward marks of inner character. Sentimental typology had provided a way to link true character with apparent character, the inner self with the social mask or disguise. (Halttunen, 189)

But that linkage of "true" and "apparent" character, over time, inevitably distorted the meaning of "true" character itself until, with consumer culture stridently on its upward curve by the late 1870s, the social self became little more than a cluster of appurtenances, a collection of masks, surfaces, and performances. For James, the most extreme form of this distortion would be portrayed in the figure of Serena Merle in *The Portrait of a Lady*.

What Felix Younger and Morris Townsend accomplish is to use their charm as a means of guaranteeing the effectiveness of these new shapes for the display of candor and sincerity. Eugenia Munster acknowledges the usefulness of that "charming nature," regarding it as "our capital" (*Europeans*, 37), and Felix himself shares this sense of charm's capacities in the marketplace: "The more charming a woman is, the more numerous, literally, are her definite social uses" (*Europeans*, 132). Townsend, whose performances are a less colorful version of what we find in Felix and, particularly, Eugenia, would not dissent from such a view; the only difference between the charm of the two men is in its respective success and failure as a social mechanism. If Felix's charm falls short of Eugenia's bright theatricality, that falling short is to reflect back upon the cult of sincerity that renders the initial New England singleness of expression (a "well-ordered consciousness" [*Europeans*, 71] organizes the Wentworth house, where "the simple details of the picture addressed themselves to the eye as distinctly as the items of a 'sum' in addition" [*Europeans*, 47]) available for the later performances sanctioned by the practices of consumption.

James's arithmetical analogy here is striking. It anticipates the more complicated mathematics used on behalf of Dr. Sloper, and for the singleness of the New England perspective that *The Europeans* associates with sincerity, it registers an interesting compact with the world of commerce. Arithmetic is entirely appropriate for a perspective that is "angular" (*Europeans*, 186), like Mr. Wentworth's "extremely neat and well-dusted" and oddly named "office" (not a study) at home (*Europeans*, 174). The text itself draws our attention to this oddity of nomenclature ("denominated, for reasons not immediately apparent") in order to suggest the complexity of the equation James is establishing between singleness of vision (Wentworth resists Felix's offer to paint him because such an act would, literally, involve a duplication of what already exists—it is a resistance to multiplicity, to otherness), sincerity, and commerce. Wentworth's domestic "office" presumably matches his place of business in Devonshire Street where, with a telling pun, "a large amount of highly confidential trust-business" is transacted (*Europeans*, 88). Terms such as *confidence* and *trust* were becoming vibrant with duplicity in the 1840s, and this particular piece of information is curious in that it is wholly unnecessary to the narrative. Its textual redundancy perhaps looks forward to another kind of shadow-iness, that of Townsend's business in *Washington Square*; here its redundancy from the point of view of the story is graphed by its being placed in parenthesis, suggesting almost an afterthought. The marginality of the item in narrative and typographical terms—enhanced by its reference to the "later years" of Wentworth's career—draws our attention by its very curiousness and redundancy. There is, too, a local oddity in that we might wonder why, if he has a "large" amount of business to transact, Wentworth, in his "later years," visits Devonshire Street "but three times a week" (*Europeans*, 88). What our attention is drawn toward is the compacted "confidential trust-business." For Wentworth, at the end of the period when *confidence* and *trust* meant what they say, the compaction is wholly unproblem-atical; but for the nexus of the period we find negotiated by *The Europeans* and *Washington Square*, the 1840s–1870s (and we might remember that Melville published *The Confidence Man* in 1857), it is, at the least, strikingly unstable—readable only as a nostalgic feature of New England's "silvery prime," open (sincere) as the door of the Wentworth house itself (*Europeans*, 51). Even Mr. Wentworth is as capable as Eugenia and Felix, or Sloper and Townsend, in a descending order of magnitude, of the language of commercial appropriation. There is, for example, his rather strange remark about Gertrude, late in the novel, on the occasion of Felix's proposal: "She has not profited as we hoped" (*Europeans*, 184).

Felix belongs within the interstitial arena between the singleness of sincerity advertised by Wentworth and the multiplicity of performance practiced by Eugenia; he inhabits, to continue with Halttunen's useful phrase, the cult of sincerity—where, for example, he can respond to Wentworth's assumptions that "moral grounds" are fixed and absolute by suggesting gently, "It is sometimes very moral to change, you know" (*Europeans*, 186). The cult developed styles of sincerity to compete with and to resist the styles of social performance; in the process, it fell prey to the glamour of style itself, to the defining feature of consumer culture. By the 1850s,

> middle-class Americans were beginning to break out of the vicious circle established by the sentimental ideal of sincerity and to embrace more avowedly theatrical cultural forms. Proper dress gradually came to be accepted as a legitimate form of disguise; proper etiquette was increasingly viewed as a means of masking and thus controlling unacceptable social impulses; and mourning ritual was coming to be a form of public theater, designed to display the perfect gentility of its participants. (Halttunen, 190)

This is the ethos toward which Felix is moving; Townsend has achieved it, and Eugenia has mastered it most completely. Eugenia's full name is Eugenia-Camilla-Dolores, the Baroness Munster of Silberstadt-Schreckenstein, and Richard Poirier is absolutely right in noting that its "suggestion of a complicated and even contradictory variety of personal roles is thoroughly appropriate to Eugenia's character and to her place in the novel" (Poirier, *100*). It is instructive that no other character in the James canon enjoys such a cornucopia of demoninative flourish. Her variousness and the performances expressing her multiplicity are what designate her and Serena Merle (her less extravagant but no less accomplished counterpart in *The Portrait of a Lady*) as figures of the 1870s, the period in which "a new success literature was emerging that effectively instructed its readers to cultivate the arts of the confidence man in order to succeed in the business world." The manipulation of others through artifice was coming to be accepted as a "necessary executive skill"; whereas antebellum advice literature had "cautioned young men never to cultivate outward appearances at the expense of inner realities," postbellum success manuals "advised their readers about how to manipulate appearances to their own advantage" (Halttunen, 198, 204).

Catherine Sloper is James's most direct portrayal of the sincere self that characterized the 1830s and 1840s. Contrasting her "uncloaked heart" and Austin Sloper's scientific rigidity (the ossifying version of her sincerity) are the factitious cultivations of Morris Townsend and Lavinia Penniman, cultivations that mark them as anticipations of those codes of manners more characteristic of the later period. James had begun to investigate the pattern of this encounter in *The Europeans* (where the contemporaneity of Eugenia's artfulness is set against the standards of earlier forms of sincerity), and he would continue to analyze it in *The Portrait of a Lady* (where the antitheses between Serena Merle and Isabel Archer serve a similar function, although lacking in the historical specificity we find in *The Europeans* and *Washington Square*). Mrs. Penniman is irritated by Catherine's lack of capacity for histrionics (*WS*, 129); her own histrionics—Mrs. Penniman is one who "always, even in conversation, italicised her personal pronouns" (*WS*, 114)—counter even the syntax of Catherine's reticence. Dramatization, even self-dramatization, is not necessarily to be condemned (as we see in Eugenia, who uses it to enriching effect), but its formulation by Mrs. Penniman moves it to a self-absorption that produces one of the greatest Jamesian sins—the exploitation of public occasions for personal ends: one of Mrs. Penniman's ideal scenarios for Catherine and Morris is "a private marriage" (*WS*, 112), a vivid distortion of a communally celebrated ceremony.

Catherine's reticence, her quietude, is the clearest expression of her sincerity, a mode that is "incapable of elaborate artifice" (*WS*, 53). Paradoxically, as Mrs. Almond, Sloper's "wiser sister," recognizes, such sincerity itself can already be a social detriment. She notes of Catherine's marital prospects: "And if our young men appear disinterested . . . it is because they marry, as a general thing, so young—before twenty-five, at the age of innocence and sincerity—before the age of calculation. If they only waited a little, Catherine would fare better" (*WS*, 61). Summarized here, in the antipathy between "innocence and sincerity" and "calculation" is the entire debate about manners that is conducted by all three novels. It is part of Catherine's tragedy that she has no "calculation," that she has no appreciation of performativeness. Such a failure may be morally laudable, but it is also socially disadvantageous. We see her dissemble rarely, but on one of those occasions her dissembling is used to highlight the ethos she represents. It is after her final, painful meeting with Townsend, and she has to protect herself from the subsequent conversation with Mrs. Penniman about her grief. Through Catherine's closed door, her aunt inquires, "Can I do anything to help you?" and she replies, "I am not in any trouble whatever, and do not need any help." The narrative instructs us here that she is "fibbing roundly, and proving thereby that not only our faults, but our most involuntary misfortunes, tend to corrupt our morals" (*WS*, 187). This instruction is a good example of the kind of judgment founded upon sincerity that James associates with the 1830s and 1840s: it is a highly sententious verdict upon a minor, and eminently understandable, white lie that we can easily imagine also being told by a figure like Mr. Wentworth. Catherine is trapped as much by the codes of sincerity as by the experiments of Sloper and the performativeness of Townsend and Mrs. Penniman.

12

Shapes of the Self—
II: Fibs and Mirrors

Catherine's fib to Mrs. Penniman is not only understandable within the immediate psychology of its occasion. It is, we might feel—to use one of the more problematic of the novel's terms—also "natural," both in the sense of her proper need for self-protection at this point and in the sense that any moral code that would condemn it is in itself paralyzing and inhuman. In this context, *The Europeans* has already begun to explore the resonance of such fibs: the white lie is a feature of Eugenia's social strategies. The world of the 1840s that images itself as one of openness, candor, and sincerity is neatly and familiarly figured by the volume of Emerson's *Essays* that lies in the sickroom of Mrs. Acton (*Europeans*, 109). Eugenia has made the relevant comment on the Bostonians with some irony a few pages earlier: "I am told they are very sincere; they don't tell fibs" (*Europeans*, 101). It is especially striking, then, that the fib she tells herself in meeting Mrs. Acton is the first one in which she is caught out, and that it should occur in the presence of a person who is "very ill," presided over by Emerson's volume. She tells Mrs. Acton that her son "has talked to me immensely of you." This is a very brief scene and one that is careful not to force self upon our attention, but it schematizes graphically the historical process registered by the novel. To Eugenia in the immediate local context, fibbing does not matter: "Who were these people to whom such fibbing was not pleasing?" she asks (*Europeans, 109*), and she is surely right. Her fib is a social pleasantry designed to ease the progress of a sticky conversation and would be a perfectly acceptable tactic of manners in the 1870s. It is not accidental that within less than a page, at the beginning of the next chapter, we are told that Felix—whom the novel allows to be much more at home in the New England society of the 1840s than Eugenia's artifice will ever permit—is "a decidedly flattering painter" (*Europeans*, 111). In deciding on the ethical scale between the "fibbing" of artifice and the "flattering" feature of the candor we associate with Felix, we enter the historicism James uses the naturalness of fibbing to explore. At the very least we recognize his paradoxical negotiations (as part of that historicism) of what may be assumed to be natural and sincere and what is conceived as artificial and performative.

Notions of "natural" feelings, desires, and behavior are tested continually throughout the novel, principally by the contemporary artfulness of Eugenia's performances. When she tells Robert Acton of the impulse for her visit to America from Europe—"I had a sort of longing to come into those natural relations which I knew I should find here. Over there, I had only, as I may say, artificial relations" (*Europeans*, 102)—she is deploying the "natural" in the service of an idea of naturalness: the "air" of the natural. I am thinking here of Jean Baudrillard's argument that, within the codes of consumer society, "natural" becomes displaced by the notion of "naturalness," and crucially for any debate about the self, "person" becomes displaced by "personality."[1] It is in this way that the sacred pillars of the natural, authenticity and sincerity, are revealed as subject to design, to the intimate intrusions of consumption's artifice. Morris Townsend's performance of the "natural" belongs exactly to this order of things. We see here the most fundamental paradox of the Jamesian enterprise. *The Europeans* is clearly committed to the style of Eugenia as ameliatory, as exploring the limitations of the New England temperament; this is a commitment to the liberation of design (the manufactured art of the world, which promises alterability—multiplicity instead of singleness of view), which is itself a function of design's system. This is why Gertrude Wentworth's outburst to the restrictive Reverend Brand is so pivotal for the novel's historicity. In defense of the "frivolous," of "pleasure" and "amusement," Gertrude proclaims: "I am trying for once to be natural. . . . I have been pretending, all my life; I have been dishonest; it is you that have made me so" (*Europeans*, 128). She repeats her position later when, in telling her equally restrictive father of her wish to marry Felix, she levels the same accusation: "You wouldn't let me be natural" (*Europeans*, 184). Gertrude's opposing of the natural to pretense in the novel's setting of the 1840s properly invokes the authority of the sincere self, the self proclaimed by Emerson's essay "Self-Reliance" (1841) and by the quietude of Catherine Sloper. But already that opposition is being threatened by the developing marketplace. If the 1840s is in part for James the period of Emersonian sincerity, it is also the period of that which sincerity is beginning to need to structure itself against—a period of dazzle and deception that Emerson describes in his less well known essay "Experience" (1844). With striking prescience, Emerson's worries about the New England culture of the 1840s and its threat to the self's integrity anticipate the effects of consumption in the 1870s.

The world of Emerson's essay is a world of surface, the displays of performance that the advertising industry, the great department stores, and the handbooks on etiquette of the 1870s would structure more vividly. "All things swim and glitter. Our life is not so much threatened as our perception. Ghostlike we glide through nature, and should not know our place again," claims Emerson about a world where "there is at last no rasping friction, but the most slippery sliding surfaces." Even the most intense experience, suffering, fails to find the sharp "friction" that might claw such surfaces: "There are moods in which we court suffering, in the hope that here at least we shall find reality, sharp peaks and edges of truth. But it turns out to be scene-painting and counterfeit. . . . That, like all the rest, plays about the surface, and never introduces me into the reality."[2] In one sense, we have here a familiar Emersonian story that opposes the relativity and subjectivity of the experienced world to the absoluteness of what he calls the "great and crescive self" ("Experience," 77), but it would be

misleading to leave that story solely within the confines of transcendentalist thought. When Emerson argues that "intellectual tasting of life
will not supersede muscular activity" ("Experience," 61), he offers an
oblique reminder of the world of labor suppressed by the commodity
relation that had already begun to inform perception during the 1830s.

Repose and stasis, the negative conditions of Catherine Sloper's
quietude, are perennial anxieties for Emerson and are tantamount to
mercantile paralysis, the abstractions of the commodity relation. In a
journal entry for 10 December 1836, he asked a question that James
would have thoroughly approved: "Do you not see that a man is a
bundle of relations, that his entire strength consists not in his properties
but in his innumerable relations?"[3] James's notions of "relations" are
among his great discoveries as a novelist, and they owe much to
Emerson. Here, the fluidity and alterability of "relations" are opposed
to the frozen, immutable qualities of "properties" as a shorthand for
a presiding argument about the deadness of a world coming to be
dominated by commercial models. A journal entry for 2 August 1837,
the year of financial panic, stated Emerson's antipathy to the "repose"
of commercial immutability with unusual clarity, a clarity impelled by
his recognition of the extent of contemporary paralysis: "I find it to
be a mischievous notion of our times that men think we are come late
into nature, that the world is finished and sealed, that the world is of
a constitution unalterable, and see not that in the hands of genius old
things are passed away and all things become new" (*Journals*, 349).
The notion of alterability is central to the lecture "Politics" (1840) as
an antidote to a commercial culture that is "monumental in its repose,"[4] and "Man the Reformer" (1841) takes its title literally to
intend man the "re-maker." Alterability is one of the main features
suppressed by the commodity relation's emptying both persons and
objects of content for the purposes of exchange (the major theme of
Washington Square). This emptying constitutes the ground for the
more pervasive evacuations of consumption (the major theme of *The
Bostonians*) that become evident during the 1870s and 1880s. The
sincerity of self-reliance in the subjective world depicted by Emerson
in "Experience"—"Thus inevitably does the universe wear our color,
and every object fall successively into the subject itself" ("Experience,"

80)—veers alarmingly close to self-centeredness, which, as *The Bosto-nians* again demonstrates, is one of consumption's worst distortions.

Emerson is deliberately various about surface. When it is opposed to depth, it belongs to illusoriness; but that is only part of the story. Not only is that opposition disavowed (again, an important Jamesian lesson), but surface itself is credited with a special reality of its own, sanctioned by modern science, as Emerson notes: "The new molecular philosophy shows astronomical interspaces betwixt atom and atom, shows that the world is all outside; it has no inside" ("Experience," 66). James's version occurs most famously in his preface to *The Awk-ward Age*, where he defines the "objectivity" of drama as an absence of any "going behind" of character to pander to a novelistic illusion of some deeper self (*French Writers*, 1131). Emerson's reconstructed reality of surface, which is fictional at the same time, is strengthened further by its alliance with the principle of change, with all that resists the more dangerous illusion of the permanent:

> The secret of the illusoriness is in the necessity of a succession of moods or objects. Gladly we would anchor, but the anchorage is quicksand. This onward trick of nature is too strong for us: *Pero si muove*. When at night I look at the moon and stars, I seem station-ary, and they to hurry. Our love of the real draws us to permanence, but health of body consists in circulation, and sanity of mind in variety or facility of association. We need change of objects. ("Expe-rience," 58)

Change, for Emerson, is associated with a sense of the alterability of things, a sense that recognizes that objects, institutions, laws, any of the governing factors of life, are *made*, are constructed by human agency at the very moment when such making is being disguised and beginning to be suppressed and forgotten by commercial practices—or, in the case of *Washington Square*, when the mobility and placeless-ness of Morris Townsend and his "natural" performances are seen by Dr. Sloper as threatening to the permanence of his world of types, as revelatory of the design of his own progress toward bourgeois success. Emerson's writings on these issues during the 1840s seem to me to powerfully inform James's conception of the novel's principal male characters (as, indeed, James's thinking in general is so often indebted to Emersonian positions). The conjunction of surface (and, by implication, performance), change, and alterability we find in "Experience" provides, in "Politics," Emerson's fullest statement on the necessity for remaking as a means of disclosing the alterable design of the state, a remaking that insists upon a view of society as "superficial" in the potent sense offered by "Experience"—as released by surface from the illusion of depth or root:

> Let us not politely forget the fact that [the state's] institutions are not aboriginal though they existed before we were born: that they are not superior to the citizen: that every one of its institutions was once a man: that every one of its laws and usages was a man's expedient to meet a particular fact: that they are all alterable, all imitable; we may make as good; we may make better. All society is an optical illusion to the young adventurer. It looks to him massive and monumental in its repose with certain names, men, institutions rooted like oak trees to the centre round which all arrange themselves the best they can and must arrange themselves. But the fact is Society is fluid; there are not such roots and centres but any monad there may instantly become the centre of the whole movement and compel the whole to gyrate around him. ("Politics," 240)

Emerson's sketch of the resistance of alterability to the seeming permanence of society is precisely what we discover in the relationships between Townsend and Sloper, and Eugenia Munster and the Wentworths. In the late 1870s surface and performance were foregrounded by consumption as part of the dazzle of spectacle and, simultaneously, were authorized by the shifts in manners and revised notions of the self as agencies for social and business intercourse. In the Emersonian 1840s they were recognized as the new reality of commercial and industrial practices through their suppressions of process, of labor and the systems of production. Simultaneously, through their alliance with the conceptions of things being made and consequently of their alterability, they became important strategies for resisting the "monumental" permanence of the new industrial age by means of their dise gagement from depth and center. It is these paradoxes we find exploited in *Washington Square, The Europeans,* and *The Portrait of a Lady* in the forms of new resonances for the "natural." They are exploited as a testimony to, and anxiety about, the reconstructed authenticity of artifice. Surface and performance increasingly governed social life by the 1870s: this was how things were experienced within the new commerce. Simultaneously, James understood how they were also a means of reconstituting essentialist, absolutist notions of the self and its behavior, which were gathered under the rubric of sincerity. This reconstitution was enabled principally by the allegiance given by surface and performance to a relational view of the world, disturbing the "repose" or stasis of established objects and manners. The performances of Townsend, Eugenia, and Serena Merle display a capacity for change and variousness against the settled positions and "types" they confront. They thus share the Emersonian ambition of the 1840s to dispel fixed social mores, and they exhibit also the main feature of contemporary consumption in the 1870s and 1880s. This entanglement tests consumption, displays the human history of its development, and, particularly in the case of Eugenia, succumbs to its glamour at the same time.

In short, James's novels give testimony to the fact that manufacture itself, understood as belonging to the world of performance and design, may reconstruct and appropriate the "natural." While Gertrude Wentworth's opposing of naturalness to pretense in the setting of the 1840s is properly authorized by the strictures of sincerity, by the time of James's writing in the late 1870s consumption had entered its new and strident phase and its terms were too fully reorganized to allow for such separation. Art may indeed make for nature, as Tony Tanner cleverly observes,[5] but in the process nature is displayed as the product of design equally with anything else in the marketplace. Against Eugenia's contemporary artifice, which employs the idea of naturalness, the Wentworths and Felix rely upon the "sincerity" of the 1840s to maintain the "natural" in its conventional sense. In both *The Europeans* and *Washington Square* James uses fibbing to explore these changes in meaning. The fib is especially useful here because it is so intimate to human behavior and because it serves the double function

of being factitious, the deceit of design, while allowing that factitiousness to be understandable and, in most cases, condoned by our
reading.

When Eugenia instructs Felix early in the novel to "tell my story
in the way that seems to you most—natural" (*Europeans* 45), her
pause is that of calculation—the calculation of the effect of that story
upon the Wentworths. The "natural" is to be incorporated as the
design of Felix's narration. Gertrude Wentworth's conversation with
Mr. Brand (*Europeans*, 128) shows how the New England "natural"
serves repression, while Eugenia's fibs, when they assume the form of
social pleasantries, can be effective precisely because they are fibs.
Eugenia's first meeting with the Wentworth daughters, Gertrude and
Charlotte, leads her to call them "pretty" and "handsome." Charlotte,
who is always to be confined by the New England ethos, "blushe[s]
quickly" and clearly feels awkward about the manner of Eugenia's
compliment. But Gertrude, the figure who will be partially released
from that ethos through her relationship with Felix, is "extremely
pleased" by its very factitiousness: "It was not the compliment that
pleased her; she did not believe it; she thought herself very plain. She
could hardly have told you the source of her satisfaction; it came from
something in the way the Baroness spoke, and it was not diminished—
it was rather deepened, oddly enough—by the young girl's disbelief"
(*Europeans*, 64). That "something" is derived from Eugenia's manner:
its hospitality to others, which suggests possibilities for extensions of
the self, for moving beyond the repressive singleness of sincerity, for
entering a more various social world where the self may be permitted
a wider range of free opportunities.

Here, the fib is enabling rather than restrictive, and it is generally
true of Eugenia's performances throughout the novel that they always
contain possibilities for social amelioration and extension. More important, her fibs reconstruct the notion of the natural in the face of a
sincerity that is felt to be prohibitive. Eugenia's principal fib is to claim
to Robert Acton, her would-be suitor, that she has sent off to Europe
the document renunciating her morganatic marriage. The occasion is
a conversation in which Acton, within the terms of what he later calls,
in anticipation of Austin Sloper, his "legitimate experimentation" (*Eu-*

ropeans, 191), is able to set "invent" against "natural" in the unquestioning opposition that is meaningful in the 1840s. It is an occasion
that begins with a fib of Acton's own. Eugenia asks, "Why have you
not been to see me?" and when Acton fails to reply, she asks, "Why
don't you answer me?" to which he responds, "I am trying to invent
an answer." When he finally comes up with his answer—"If I had
done as I liked I would have come to see you several times"—she
queries, "Is that invented?" and Acton returns, "No, that is natural. I
stayed away because—." The pause is necessary for the further calculation of his invention, which then emerges as, "Because I wanted to
think about you." The invention is not lost on Eugenia, who highlights
its factitiousness with a telling pun: "Because you wanted to lie
down! . . . I have seen you lie down—almost—in my drawing-room"
(*Europeans*, 170). It is a pun that picks up further resonance from the
earlier conversation between the two on "natural" and "artificial"
relations; that talk is also concluded by a pun. There, the pun again
draws out Acton's ulterior motives: he observes that "there is one way
in which the relation of a lady and a gentleman may always become
natural," and Eugenia rejoins, "You mean by their becoming lovers?
That may be natural or not" (*Europeans*, 102–3).

The project of "experimentation," legitimate or otherwise, is to
test: Acton's feeling that "she is not honest, she is not honest," becomes, "She is a woman who will lie." It is the manipulation of the
experiment that produces the "lie," and before her simple yes in reply
to his question about the document of renunciation, Eugenia "hesi-
tated for a single moment—very naturally" (*Europeans*, 171). Her
hesitation, emphasized by the typographical pause, is "natural" on
behalf of her "lie"; it is appropriate to her calculation of duplicity.
In effect, given the situation Acton constructs for her, it is precisely
"natural" for her to "lie." The movement in this conversation from
the schism between "invent" and "natural" to the naturalness of lying
renders the "natural" as, above all, a social tactic. Both Acton's experimentation and Eugenia's performance convey that manufactured quality whereby the "natural" reveals its element of design.

Fibs are not unlike mirrors. Both require a restructuring of the
oppositional relationship between the natural and the artificial; both

incorporate the calculation of design; both display an alertness to the necessity for performance, to the variousness of otherness, which the singleness of sincerity has difficulties in acknowledging. In *Washington Square* (as we have seen in chapter 7) James uses the mirror as a complex image for the historical sense and for his practice of writing. In *The Europeans* this image is extended to provide the ground for the novel's crucial debate about perception, a debate that in its turn continues the issue of the changing forms of the self registered by the historical nexus of the 1840s–1870s. Again, *The Europeans* serves here as a companion-piece to *Washington Square* in that its concern with ways of looking closely approximates to the relationship between the naturalness of Morris Townsend's performances (offset against the more evident factitiousness of Mrs. Penniman's) and the sincerity of Catherine Sloper's quietude.

Early in *The Europeans* we are told that Felix "was in love, indiscriminately, with three girls at once," and in the midst of his fairly lumpen attempts to discriminate between the Wentworth girls, Gertrude and Charlotte, and Lizzie Acton, the narrative presents our lesson: "He had known, fortunately, many virtuous gentlewomen, but it now appeared to him that in his relations with them . . . he had been looking at pictures under glass. He perceived at present what a nuisance the glass had been—how it perverted and interfered, how it caught the reflexion of other objects and kept you walking from side to side" (*Europeans*, 81). Felix is making the distinction that grounds the novel's entire debate about perception: a distinction between an implied naturalness of looking (as direct, single, true, "in the right light") and the artifice of designed sight (as indirect, various, incorporating the otherness that always hovers on the margins of the eye's range). While Felix is discomforted by the variousness of the glass, Eugenia, in the novel's first scene, uses the mirror not only for self-decoration but for recognizing the self as other through her changing moods—for the multiplicity that is to be a "nuisance" for Felix:

> She never dropped her eyes upon his [Felix's] work; she only turned them, occasionally, as she passed, to a mirror suspended above a toilet-table on the other side of the room. Here she paused a mo-

ment, gave a pinch to her waist with her two hands, or raised these members—they were very plump and pretty—to the multifold braids of her hair, with a movement half-caressing, half-corrective. An attentive observer might have fancied that during these periods of desultory self-inspection her face forgot its melancholy; but as soon as she neared the window again it began to proclaim that she was a very ill-pleased woman. (*Europeans*, 33–34)

Eugenia's braids are the telling detail here as a constituent part of that more exotic otherness that stamps her style: her hair is "always braided in a manner that suggested some Southern or Eastern, some remotely foreign, woman" (*Europeans*, 35). It is entirely appropriate that the mirror into which Eugenia gazes at the end of the novel provides a prompt for a metaphor from the theatre (*Europeans*, 192).

If the Jamesian mirror offers images for history and for performativeness, it includes within both an allusion to the form of the romance James finds so valuable in Hawthorne as a ground for his own writing practice. Hawthorne uses the mirror to strategic effect in his reworking of Coleridge in "The Custom-House" section of *The Scarlet Letter*, written at the end of the decade that provides the setting for *The Europeans* and *Washington Square*. There, he makes his famous complaint about the atmosphere of the customhouse being so little conducive to "the delicate harvest of fancy and sensibility"; in this atmosphere, "my imagination was a tarnished mirror." His description of the imaginative faculty is dependent entirely upon images of reflection from bright surfaces through the play of diverse lights, and it concludes:

> Glancing at the looking-glass, we behold—deep within its haunted verge—the smouldering glow of the half-extinguished anthracite, the white moonbeams on the floor, and a repetition of all the gleam and shadow of the picture, with one remove farther from the actual, and nearer to the imaginative. Then, at such an hour, and with this scene before him, if a man, sitting all alone, cannot dream strange things, and make them look like truth, he need never try to write romances.[6]

Hawthorne's mirror, its image of writing and its proclamation of light's variousness, is wholly apt for the otherness discovered in Eugenia's mirror, and it points up the limitations that accrue to the single, straightforward sunlight sought by the sincerity of Felix's model of looking, a model that, in its turn, carries echoes of the "broad and simple daylight" of New England that Hawthorne both admires and regrets in his preface to *The Marble Faun*.[7] Felix's sincerity may respond primarily to a directness of vision, but like Gertrude, who had earlier found pleasure in the "something in the way the Baroness spoke" (*Europeans*, 64), in the style of Eugenia's factitiousness, he is able to respond also to the "moonlight" of the "surface" she designs. The language of his response echoes that of Hawthorne: "His sister, to his spiritual vision, was always like the lunar disk when only a part of it is lighted. The shadow on this bright surface seemed to him to expand and to contract; but whatever its proportions, he always appreciated the moonlight" (*Europeans*, 155).

What Eugenia does in front of the mirror is to identify herself as a producer of effects, a calculator of social design. Such production and calculation are, as Jean-Christophe Agnew has shown, among the main characteristics of a consumer culture.[8] The self not as origin but as effect, as a "personality" in Jean Baudrillard's sense, recognizes its place in a world it has not made. But, by the enabling paradox that I suspect James was alone in understanding during the later years of the nineteenth century, the self recognizes also that, as an effect, it retains the liberating possibility of further manufacture, which may turn out to be transformative. Eugenia's mirror thus locates both the narcissistic prison of the consumer world and its paradoxical potential for liberation by an acknowledgment of alterability. The mirror's revelation of the self as other animates the strangeness of things. This strangeness, which is familiar at the same time, is a necessary precondition for recognizing the design of things and hence for realizing their alterable nature. Paradoxically, then, the defamiliarizing impact of the mirror may enable a return to the material world of production that is otherwise repressed by consumptive perception and the commodity relati. The designed self is thus both prison and possibility, just as Cath Sloper's quietude is both sincerity and paralysis.

By reading *Washington Square* and *The Europeans* as r companion-pieces in the strictest sense of the term, we ap full complexity of James's apprehension of the situation c toward the end of the nineteenth century. James was alone among the major American novelists (and, indeed, among most of his European counterparts) in recognizing the female as the site in which the most intimate effects of contemporary culture could be explored. Catherine and Eugenia are not conceived separately but envisaged together as aspects of the same cultural tradition: we cannot understand the sincerity of the one without the performativeness of the other. It is not accidental that in James the great stylists of the self are invariably female and not male, nor that James's concern with the new social realism of artifice, of the self's representations, is powerfully bound up with his writerly practice.

13

Living in the Marketplace

With the aid of *The Europeans* as an indispensable lens through which to consider the preoccupations of *Washington Square*, I have been notating the cultural impulses that animate James's choice of the 1830s and 1840s as the setting for both novels from the point of view of the late 1870s. By way of conclusion, I want to give a more general consideration to the tactics involved in this most singular expression of James's historical sense and its aesthetic determinants.

Mathematics, the calculability that sanctions Sloper's placing of Townsend's "category" and his estimate of Catherine's "value," provides the basis for both the types of science and the prices of the marketplace. The uniformity imposed by both depends upon laws of the repeatable and the imperishable, figuring absolutes of time and space so that, in Alfred Sohn-Rethel's accurate phrase, "time becomes unhistorical time and space ungeographical space" (Sohn-Rethel, 49 56). A substantial part of *Washington Square's* historicism is to def this possibility by its relativistic deployment of the periods of its se and composition. Simultaneously, however, it does not wish prey to the confining factualism of realistic fiction and so ins play with its temporal and topographical resources: it is most striking features of the novel that it progressively dissolves both time and space, those two essential properties of realistic fiction's aids to illusion.

The Square itself, by means of its topographical density and the unusual care James takes with temporal specification in the opening chapters, is categorically offered as a retreat from the bedlam of commerce. Curiously, however, with the development of the story the rest of the city becomes more and more evasive as an explicit context for the narrative. We see this in the pattern of increasing anonymity that characterizes the locations chosen by Mrs. Penniman for her private meetings with Townsend outside the definiteness of the Square: they move from "an oyster saloon in the Seventh Avenue" (WS, 109), through the doorstep of a church that is a "less elegant resort" than her usual place of worship (WS, 138), to a "street corner, in a region of empty lots and undeveloped pavements" (WS, 174). As a locale, the Square is felt gradually to lose its relational contact with the city, and it is in this sense that its space becomes ungeographical—matching, perhaps, the self-sealing tenets of Sloper's perspective.

When we examine the novel's time scheme, we find that its chronology is conflicting.[1] There are, for example, three competing sets of dates established in the opening three chapters for the commencement of the story's action: 1843, 1846, and 1838 or 1839. Equally, there are three competing dates for its termination in the final meeting of Catherine and Townsend: 1851 or 1852, 1856, and 1859. Furthermore, this computation ignores the fact that a character's age and a date are conjoined only once: we are told that Sloper married at the age of 27 in 1820 (WS, 28). So when he dies in chapter 33, "touching his seventieth year," the date must be 1862 or 1863, making the terminal date for the action 1863 or 1864. The novel also provides more domestic versions of its wider chronological conflict. Catherine lies and Townsend is evasive about the time of their first meeting (WS, 4, 88–89), and there is a discrepancy over the ages of Sloper's sisters: . Almond is first cited as "younger" (WS, 31), but later as the —" (WS, 58). The conclusion we need to draw is clear: not only faced with sets of dates that compete among themselves, but competition is inconsistent. The narrative's offering of dates and ages only at the beginning and the end, framing an un-timed middle where the bulk of the action occurs, underlines James's willingness to defuse determinant chronology. His dissolve of the specific dates themselves renders that willingness a purposive tactic of historical removal. Such removal exploits those features of the bourgeois temperament we have already noted: the obscuring of process in order to maintain uniformity and universality, the characteristics of commodity abstraction within the network of exchange. What needs stressing is the approximation, not the matching, of James's tactic to these features.

James is writing at the beginning of the second great phase of commercial expansion in America, a phase that expressed vividly and in large outline those forms of corporate capitalism that structured New York in the period of the novel's setting. The America James left behind in 1875 lay in the middle of the depression that followed the gold panic of 1869. During the years immediately prior to composing *Washington Square* he was surrounded by the development of a disengaged, abstractive system of commercial and financial behavior that displayed on a large canvas the outcome of its birth in the 1830s and 1840s. It was a period in which the truth of the Emersonian lesson in his father's "Socialism and Civilization" (1849) became contemporaneously accurate: "We degrade by owning and just in the degree of our owning . . . We degrade and disesteem every person we own absolutely, every person bound to us by any other tenure than his own spontaneous affection."[2] Writing from Europe, James regretted, in a letter of December 1877, the declining political prestige of England and expressed the patrician hope that the country would show itself to be more than "one vast, money-getting Birmingham" (*Letters II*, 145). And around the time of composition itself, he wrote tellingly, in January 1879, of a trip to the North: "Yorkshire smoke-country is very ugly and depressing, both as regards the smirched and blackened landscape and the dense and dusky population, who form a not v attractive element in that grand total of labour and poverty on w enormous base all the luxury and leisure of English country-are built up" (*Letters II*, 209). A year later, as part of his i disillusionment with the vacuousness of the English social noted: "The country is in a very dismal state—everyone poor" (*Letters II*, 261).

When we acknowledge the approximation between James's dissolving of time and space in *Washington Square* and the features of the marketplace, we acknowledge also the extent of his own site within it. Catherine undeniably focuses much of our sympathy, and if her quietude, her paralyzed speech, espouses the frozen abstraction that is her fate as a commodity, it is also advertised as a gesture of innocence and sincerity against a shabby and loquacious materialism. As we have seen, sincerity was a meaningful social compact in the 1840s, but by the 1870s and 1880s, the period of Eugenia Munster and of Isabel Archer's struggle on this very issue with Serena Merle, it had been severely disabled as a social maneuver. Nevertheless, as the experience of *Washington Square* shows us, it still retained a potential to counter the excesses of the commercial world. That is why James remained willing to pursue it in the form of the "fine consciousness" he would try to develop in *The Portrait of a Lady*. Such "consciousness," as we see in the portrayal of Isabel Archer or, later, in the transcendental triumph of Milly Theale in *The Wings of the Dove*, is only possible through removals from material urgencies, from economic necessities. If Catherine's quietude represents a kind of triumph over the balanced worlds of Sloper and Townsend and the fantastical romanticizing of Mrs. Penniman, then it is a triumph after the event—a means of appropriation from the placid contentment of the "morsel of fancywork" with which she ends the novel in her front parlor. At the same time, however, her quietude does register James's impulse to effect his own resistance to a "vast, money-getting" world: by locating the less oppressive and less visible features of the Gilded Age in the period of its nascence, the novel is, in part at least, attempting an act of salvation from its squalid excesses.

In this sense, we can read the novel as an attempt to salvage ~sibilities for fuller, more communal, more organic living in order ~ercome the divisive life imposed by commodity production. The ~n is that this form of romanticism involves the same contradic- ~witness in Catherine's quietude, which articulates both the ~mes's anxiety (its paralyzed, nondialogical incapacity) and the flawed alternative to it (an increasingly difficult gesture toward authenticity and sincerity, and a freedom from lexical and institutional impositions). In other words, sincerity is obliged to assume the very terms of its opposition. As Terry Eagleton notes on behalf of England (with Thomas Carlyle, Matthew Arnold, and John Ruskin in mind): "As Victorian capitalism assumes increasingly corporate forms, it turns to the social and aesthetic organicism of the Romantic humanist tradition, discovering in art models of totality and affectivity relevant to its ideological requirements" (Eagleton, 103). And in America the flowering of romanticism occurred at the very moment marked by the rupture between private and corporate systems of production—the 1830s, *Washington Square*'s setting. Emerson's great early treatises all appeared shortly after the time of Dr. Sloper's move to Washington Square: *Nature* in 1836, "The American Scholar" in 1837, the Divinity School "Address" in 1838, and "Self-Reliance" in 1841. Many of the transcendentalist positions advertised themselves as removed from the world of public affairs, but they certainly shared crucial aspects of Jacksonian reformism, particularly in the area of economic life, where transcendentalists saw the new forms of capital and commerce expressly threatening individual liberty. The rise of a new monied class (a rise that accelerated during the Gilded Age, in the figures of E. H. Harriman and the elder J. P. Morgan, for example) undermined the principles of equality and self-sufficiency that are fundamental to a democratic culture and, by the late 1870s, succeeded in translating the notion of individual liberty into the liberty of laissez-faire capitalism to engage in the profit-making of the national and international markets.

Although James clearly sympathizes with the tenets of transcendentalist resistance (as we see in the positive aspect of Catherine's quietude), the historical maneuvering of *Washington Square* and *The Europeans* dissuades us from reading his project as an unproblematic salvaging of fine consciousness from the ravages of vulgar materialism (and this is a further reason for reading the two novels *together*). It this maneuvering that should also dissuade us from the kind of con sion that Eagleton reaches (exemplifying a critical position as by commentators over the entire range of political persuasion

James's work is removed from concrete history on the grounds that it displaces those material conflicts for the wealth that renders such consciousness possible (Eagleton, 141–45). Certainly we witness no "material conflicts" in the form of novelistic realism and the historicism that accompanies it, but, as I have been trying to suggest, James's notion of fiction and its responsibility toward the social world belongs to a different order. Nevertheless, Eagleton does have an expressive term for the question of consciousness in James's work (although he is thinking of the later novels). This term is " 'positive' negation" (Eagleton, 142), and it may be applied usefully to the double figuration of Catherine's quietude as paralysis and sincerity. Positivity reveals her historical resistance to commerce, while negativity belongs to the danger of a transcendentalism that, in some forms, seeks to eschew material history as simply inhibiting—through its institutional shapes, for example—for the development of the authentic self. But the point is that these positions are not self-cancelling. In fact, it is at their intersection that James's historicism finds its most potent expression through the interplay of the two periods in American history that constitute the novel's cultural meaning.

The tensile nexus of this interplay is what informs *Washington Square*'s dissolve of time and space, which produces not "unhistorical" time or "ungeographical" space but the interstices of time and space in recognition of process itself—the changes witnessed by the periods of setting and composition. The dissolving tactics of the novel match the transformational aspect of the city itself, which, as Arthur Townsend observes, is "growing so quick." The imperative here is "to keep up with it" (*WS*, 50), but such keeping up requires an alarming array of new habits and new manners; they are filled with possibility but fraught with instability as the older reassurances are dispelled by the necessities of performance. In Philip Fisher's useful phrase, the city is but "half-built":

> The city is unstable, not only in the sense of being only partially built, but more importantly because it includes the dynamic assump-
> ion of individual fortunes that hold out the possibility of rising to
> top or failing to rise, falling or losing one's footing. Not the

family, but the individual is the central actor within the privileged setting of the city. Neither moral choices nor patterns of manners, but careers give the scheme of action.[3]

The self who will survive within such dynamic uncertainty, who will most successfully negotiate its dispersals and transformations, will be the self who is able to exploit variousness and multiplicity rather than the singleness associated with sincerity—in short, the performative self. The prime figure for such variousness is the actress, as James will acknowledge implicitly in the character of Verena Tarrant in *The Bostonians* and explicitly in that of Miriam Rooth in *The Tragic Muse* (1890). But already that figure is recognized at the time of *Washington Square* in *The Europeans'* Eugenia Munster and in *The Portrait of a Lady*'s Serena Merle, characters who display a variety of roles all of which are geared to the merchandising requirements of the markets they inhabit. Within this world of possibilities that are always temporary, the very solidity of the resistance we see in Catherine Sloper is itself illusory in that it confines her to paralysis as much as she is confined by the experimentation of her father and by the moment of change in manners, in the means of social display. The variousness that was beginning to characterize life in the city during the 1840s is registered by the interstices I have been outlining—most obviously in the novel's temporal and geographical dissolutions, but also in its presentation of social and personal intercourse. Note, for example, how many conversations, usually at important moments, take place in the vicinity of doors, the intersective points of the house's internal topography, and how often hands seem poised on doorknobs at these moments. Such placings effectively picture the modernity of James's historical sense, the liminality we see in his distrust of the center in favor of those more radical hoverings on the margins of events—or rooms.

James's attempt to "know" the offensiveness of the Gilded Age in *Washington Square* and *The Europeans* locates its origins historically in order to exploit the extent to which his own discourse belongs to the ideological equipment of that which it opposes. The historical relativism exhibited in his play with an American past may thus be to have a crucial role within his concomitant concerns, particularly in *Hawthorne*, with the nature of fiction and the production of writing. By reading Catherine Sloper and Eugenia Munster together, we can see how James attempts an imaginative and romantic (in Hawthorne's sense) rewriting of the commodity form by stressing its glamour (in the case of Eugenia), uniqueness, and resistance to confinement (in the case of both Eugenia and Catherine). He aestheticizes the commercial object of the late 1870s within the earlier history of the 1840s in order to display the extent to which an unconscious valorization of the terms he associates with his double reading of commodities (quietude and artful performativeness) perpetuates those terms in an apparently innocent manner. Catherine's quietude and Eugenia's artfulness provide grounds for questioning the bourgeois respectability of Sloper and the Wentworths, and thus also the nascence of the American commercial expansion that commenced its more visible phase in the 1870s. But at the same time such quietude and artfulness are obliged to assume the features whereby that respectability will achieve commercial success in the age of consumption. The major issues of multiplicity and singleness I have been describing are not far removed from the relation of the romance to the novel, a relation in which the imagination (in both its quiet and its extravagant forms) seeks to establish itself as an arena for interrogating and interpreting the apparent givens of factuality, realism, and history. James's achievement is to display how the tactics of that interpretation, renegotiating the "old" and the "new" within a more complex version of Hawthorneque "latitude," not only comment upon but reproduce history.

NOTES AND REFERENCES

Chapter 1

1. Richard Chase, *The American Novel and Its Tradition* (New York: Doubleday Anchor, 1957), 12–13.

2. Leon Edel, ed., *Henry James Letters, 1875–1883*, vol. 2 (Cambridge, Mass: Belknap Press of Harvard University Press, 1975), 240, hereafter cited in text as *Letters II*.

Chapter 2

1. Wallace Stevens, "Of Modern Poetry", *The Collected Poems of Wallace Stevens* (London: Faber and Faber, 1966), 239–40.

2. Henry James, *Hawthorne* (London: Macmillan, 1967), 61.

Chapter 3

1. Roger Gard, ed., *Henry James: The Critical Heritage* (London: Routledge and Kegan Paul, 1968), 550, hereafter cited in text.

2. See Darshan Singh Maini, "*Washington Square*: A Centennial Essay," *Henry James Review* 1, no.2 (Spring 1979): 86, hereafter cited in text.

3. Rebecca West, *Henry James* (London: Nisbet and Co., 1916), 55–56.

4. Ezra Pound, "Henry James," in *Literary Essays of Ezra Pound*, ed. T. S. Eliot (London: Faber and Faber, 1960), 307, hereafter cited in text.

5. Cornelia Pulsifer Kelley, *The Early Development of Henry James*, rev. ed. (1930; Urbana: University of Illinois Press, 1965), 280–83.

6. F. O. Matthiessen, *Henry James: The Major Phase* (1944; New Yor Oxford University Press, 1963), 122.

7. *The American Novels and Stories of Henry James*, ed. F. O. Matt

sen (1947; New York: Alfred A. Knopf, 1964), xv; hereafter cited in text as *Novels and Stories*.

8. Leon Edel, *The Life of Henry James*, 2 vols. (Harmondsworth: Penguin Books, 1977), II: 590–92, hereafter cited in text.

9. Alfred Habegger, *Gender, Fantasy, and Realism in American Literature* (New York: Columbia University Press, 1982), and *Henry James and the "Woman Business"* (Cambridge: Cambridge University Press, 1989).

10. Mary Doyle Springer, *A Rhetoric of Literary Character: Some Women of Henry James* (Chicago: University of Chicago Press, 1978), 81, hereafter cited in text.

11. F. W. Dupee, *Henry James* (New York: William Sloane Associates, 1951), 65, hereafter cited in text.

12. F. R. Leavis, *The Great Tradition* (1948; Harmondsworth: Penguin Books, 1967), 154.

13. Maxwell Geismar, *Henry James and the Jacobites* (Boston: Houghton Mifflin, 1963), 37, hereafter cited in text.

14. James W. Gargano, "*Washington Square*: A Study in the Growth of an Inner Self," *Studies in Short Fiction* 13, no.3 (Summer 1976): 355.

15. Richard B. Hovey, "*Washington Square*: James and 'The Deeper Psychology,' " *Hartford Studies in Literature* 14, no.1 (Fall 1982): 8, hereafter cited in text.

16. Robert Emmet Long, "James's *Washington Square*: The Hawthorne Relation," *New England Quarterly* 46, no.4 (December 1973): 573–90; Harold Schechter, "The Unpardonable Sin in *Washington Square*," *Studies in Short Fiction* 10, no.2 (Spring 1973): 137–41; Thaddeo K. Babiiha, "James's *Washington Square*: More on the Hawthorne Relation," *Nathaniel Hawthorne Journal* 4, no.3 (Summer 1974): 270–72.

17. L. C. Knights, "Henry James and Human Liberty," *Sewanee Review* 83, no.1 (Winter 1978): 17, hereafter cited in text.

18. Terry Eagleton, *Criticism and Ideology* (London: New Left Books, 1976), 141; hereafter cited in text.

19. Richard Poirier, *The Comic Sense of Henry James* (London: Chatto and Windus, 1960), 165–66, hereafter cited in text.

20. Peter Buitenhuis, *The Grasping Imagination: The American Writings of Henry James* (Toronto: University of Toronto Press, 1970), 107–8.

21. John Lucas, "*Washington Square*," in *The Air of Reality: New Essays on Henry James*, ed. John Goode (London: Methuen, 1972), 37, hereafter cited in text.

22. Millicent Bell, "Style as Subject: *Washington Square*," *Sewanee Review*, 83, no.1 (Winter 1978): 19, 38, hereafter cited in text.

23. Stuart Hutchinson, *Henry James: An American as Modernist* (London: Vision Press, 1982), 11, hereafter cited in text.

Notes and References

Chapter 4

1. T. S. Eliot, "The Hawthorne Aspect," *Little Review* (August 1918), reprinted in *The Shock of Recognition*, ed. Edmund Wilson (London: W. H. Allen, 1956), 861.

2. Henry James, *Washington Square* (Harmondsworth: Penguin Books, 1984), 27, hereafter cited in text as *WS*.

3. Henry James, *The American*, ed. James W. Tuttleton (New York: W. W. Norton, 1978), 17.

4. Henry James, "The Art of Fiction," in *Essay on Literature, American Writers, English Writers* (New York: Library of America, 1984), 53, hereafter cited in text as *Essays*.

5. Tony Tanner, "Introduction," in Henry James, *Hawthorne* ed. Tony Tanner (London: Macmillan, 1967), 2, hereafter cited in text as *Hawthorne*.

6. For bibliographical information on the relationship between *Washington Square* and Hawthorne's works, see Thaddeo K. Babiiha, *The James-Hawthorne Relation* (Boston: G. K. Hall 1980), 264–66.

7. Henry James, review of *Middlemarch* in *Essays*, 965–66.

8. Henry James, *French Writers, Other European Writers, The Prefaces to the New York Edition* (New York: Library of America, 1984), 1131, hereafter cited in text as *French Writers*.

9. Leo Bersani, "The Jamesian Lie," *Partisan Review* 36, no.1 (Winter 1969): 54, hereafter cited in text.

10. Nathaniel Hawthorne, *The House of the Seven Gables*, in *The Centenary Edition of the Works of Nathaniel Hawthorne*, ed. William Charvat, Roy Harvey Pearce, and Claude M. Simpson (Columbus: Ohio State University Press, 1965), 1–3, hereafter cited in text as *Gables*.

11. Taylor Stoehr, "Words and Deeds in *The Princess Casamassima*," *English Literary History* 37, no.1 (March 1970): 132, hereafter cited in text.

12. Leon Edel, ed., *Henry James Letters, 1883–1895*, vol.3 (Cambridge, Mass.: Belknap Press of Harvard University Press, 1980), 68–70, hereafter cited in text as *Letters III*.

13. Nathaniel Hawthorne, *The Marble Faun*, in *The Centenary Edition of the Works of Nathaniel Hawthorne*, ed. William Charvat, Roy Harvey Pearce, and Claud M. Simpson (Columbus: Ohio State University Press, 1968), 3.

14. William Dean Howells, "James's *Hawthorne*," *Atlantic Month* (February 1880), reprinted in *William Dean Howells as Critic*, ed. Edwin Cady (London: Routledge and Kegan Paul, 1973), 54.

15. Brook Thomas, "*The House of the Seven Gables*: Reading t mance of America," *PMLA* 97, no.2 (March 1982): 199.

16. Leon Edel and Lyall H. Powers eds. *The Complete Not*

Henry James (New York and Oxford: Oxford University Press, 1987), 11–12, hereafter cited in text as *Notebooks*.

Chapter 5

1. Douglas T. Miller, *Jacksonian Aristocracy: Class and Democracy in New York 1830–1860* (New York: Oxford University Press, 1967), 70–71; hereafter cited in text.

2. Douglass C. North, *The Economic Growth of the United States 1790–1860* (New York: W. W. Norton, 1966), 205.

3. Edward Pessen, *Jacksonian America: Society, Personality and Politics*, rev. ed. (Homewood, Ill: Dorsey Press, 1978), 102–3, hereafter cited in text.

4. Peter Conrad, *The Art of the City: Views and Versions of New York* (Oxford and New York: Oxford University Press, 1984), 26.

5. See Michael Feldberg's accurately entitled *The Turbulent Era: Riot and Disorder in Jacksonian America* (New York: Oxford University Press, 1980); see also Leonard L. Richards, *"Gentlemen of Property and Standing": Anti-Abolition Mobs in Jacksonian America* (New York: Oxford University Press, 1970).

6. Quoted in James F. Richardson, *The New York Police: Colonial Times to 1901* (New York: Oxford University Press, 1970), 26, 27.

7. Henry James, *The American Scene* (London: Macmillan, 1907), 100–101.

8. Thorstein Veblen, *The Theory of the Leisure Class* (1899; London: Unwin Books, 1970), 75.

9. Roland Barthes, "Myth Today," in *Mythologies*, trans. Annette Lavers (St. Albans, Herts.: Paladin, 1973), 152–53, hereafter cited in text.

10. Alfred Sohn-Rethel, *Intellectual and Manual Labour: A Critique of Epistemology*, trans. Martin Sohn-Rethel (London: Macmillan, 1978), 132–33, 112–13, 125, hereafter cited in text.

Chapter 6

1. Theodor Adorno and Max Horkheimer, *Dialectic of Enlightenment*, trans. John Cumming (London: New Left Books, 1979), 7, 31, hereafter cited in text.

2. Marc Shell, "The Gold Bug," *Genre* 13, no. 1 (Spring 1980): 18, later cited in text. The phrase about the "interplay of money and mere" is from Fernand Braudel, *Capitalism and Material Life, 1400–1800*, trans. Miriam Kochan (New York: Harper & Row, 1975), 357–58.

Notes and References

3. James Roger Sharp, *The Jacksonians Versus the Banks* (New York: Columbia University Press, 1970), 5, 6, hereafter cited in text.

For further discussions of the Jacksonian bank debate, see Bray Hammond, *Banks and Politics in America: From the Revolution to the Civil War* (Princeton, N.J.: Princeton University Press, 1957); Marvin Meyers, *The Jacksonian Persuasion.* (Stanford, Calif.: Stanford University Press, 1957); Robert V. Remini, *Andrew Jackson and the Bank War* (New York: W. W. Norton, 1967); Peter Temin, *The Jacksonian Economy* (New York: W. W. Norton, 1969).

4. William Leggett, "Equality," *New York Evening Post* (6 December 1834), reprinted in *Builders of American Institutions: Readings in United States History*, ed. Frank Freidel and Norman Pollack (Chicago: Rand-McNally, 1966), 157–58.

5. Andrew Jackson, "Farewell Address," reprinted in Freidel and Pollack, *Builders of American Institutions*, 156, hereafter cited in text as "Farewell."

6. Andrew Jackson, "Bank Veto," reprinted in William Macdonald, ed., *Select Documents Illustrative of the History of the United States 1776–1861* (New York and London: Macmillan, 1898), 262.

7. Andrew Jackson, "Fifth Annual Message," reprinted in Macdonald, *Select Documents*, 301–2.

8. Jan W. Dietrichson, *The Image of Money in the American Novel of the Gilded Age* (New York: Humanities Press, 1969), 10, hereafter cited in text.

9. Jay Martin, *Harvests of Change: American Literature 1865–1914* (Englewood Cliffs, N.J.: Prentice-Hall, 1967), 11.

10. Walter T. K. Nugent, *The Money Question during Reconstruction* (New York: W. W. Norton, 1967), 16–17, hereafter cited in text.

11. Richard Hofstadter, "Free Silver and the Mind of 'Coin' Harvey," in *The Paranoid Style in American Politics* (New York: Vintage Books, 1967), 238–39. Hofstadter's essay deals mainly with the "Free Silver" campaigns of the 1890s but offers a brief and readable account of monetary events during the 1870s (250–57).

12. Irwin Unger, *The Greenback Era: A Social and Political History of American Finance 1865–1879* (Princeton, N.J.: Princeton University Press, 1967), 3, hereafter cited in text.

Unger may be paired with Robert P. Sharkey (*Money, Class, and Pa* *An Economic Study of the Civil War and Reconstruction* [Baltimore, Johns Hopkins University Press, 1967]) in providing the most detail reliable guides to the history of money during the period. Both a' excellent bibliographies of the massive literature concerned with t'

13. See B. J. Williams, "*Washington Square*: Fiction as Hi Dissertation, University of Keele, 1983).

Chapter 7

1. In the short story "An International Episode," published shortly before *Washington Square (Cornhill* [December 1878–Januray 1879]), James presents a clear picture of the pressures within New York's commercial world.

2. Gerald T. Dunne, *Justice Story and the Rise of the Supreme Court* (New York: Simon and Schuster, 1970), 142.

3. Brook Thomas, *Cross-Examinations of Law and Literature* (Cambridge: Cambridge University Press, 1987), 84–85.

4. See Ian F. A. Bell, "The Hard Currency of Words: Emerson's Fiscal Metaphor in *Nature*," *English Literary History* 52, no. 3 (Fall 1985): 733–53.

5. Ralph Waldo Emerson, *Nature*, in *The Collected Works of Ralph Waldo Emerson*, vol. 1, ed. R. E. Spiller and A. R. Ferguson (Cambridge, MA: Belknap Press of Harvard University Press, 1971), 20, hereafter cited in text as *Nature*.

Chapter 8

1. Mark Le Fanu, "Introduction," *Washington Square*, World's Classics edition (Oxford and New York: Oxford University Press, 1982), viii, ix.

2. V. N. Volosinov, *Marxism and the Philosophy of Language*, trans. Ladislav Matejka and I. R. Titunik (New York: Seminar Press, 1973), 57–58, hereafter cited in text.

3. Richard Godden, "Some Slight Shifts in the Manner of the Novel of Manners," in *Henry James: Fiction as History*, ed. Ian F. A. Bell (London and Totowa, N.J.: Vision Press and Barnes and Noble, 1984), 169.

Chapter 9

1. Herman Melville, *Billy Budd and Other Tales* (New York: New American Library, 1961), 64.

2. *The Complete Poems of Emily Dickinson*, ed. Thomas H. Johnson (Boston: Little, Brown, 1960), 602.

3. I am grateful to my postgraduate student Jackie Vickers for making this point during a tutorial discussion.

Chapter 10

See, for example, Poirier, *The Comic Sense of Henry James*, 178.

A. Ward, "Henry James's America: Versions of Oppression," *Misterly* 13, no.1 (Winter 1959–60):40.

3. Robert R. Johannsen, "Two Sides of Washington Square," *South Carolina Review* 7, no.1 (April 1974):63.

4. William Kenney, "Dr. Sloper's Double in *Washington Square*," *University Review—Kansas City* 36, no.3 (Summer 1970): 301.

5. Henry James, *The Europeans* (Harmondsworth: Penguin Books, 1984), 52, hereafter cited in text as *Europeans*.

6. This is a point usefully touched upon by Springer (81–85).

7. Henry James, *The Bostonians* (Harmondsworth: Penguin Books, 1966), 70.

8. Norman Sidney Buck, *The Development of the Organization of Anglo-American Trade 1800–1850* (Hamden, Conn.: Archon Books, 1969), 16.

Chapter 11

1. Karen Halttunen, *Confidence Men and Painted Women: A Study of Middle-Class Culture in America, 1830–1870* (New Haven: Yale University Press, 1982), 188; hereafter cited in text.

Chapter 12

1. Jean Baudrillard, *The Mirror of Production*, trans. Mark Poster (St. Louis: Telos Press, 1975), chap. 2. For a good recent discussion and application of Baudrillard's argument, see Rachel Bowlby, *Just Looking: Consumer Culture in Dreiser, Gissing, and Zola* (London: Methuen, 1985), 25–26.

2. Ralph Waldo Emerson, "Experience," in *Essays: Second Series* (London: George Routledge and Sons, 1898), 49, 51–52, hereafter cited in text as "Experience."

3. Merton Sealts, ed., *The Journals and Miscellaneous Notebooks of Ralph Waldo Emerson*, vol.5 (Cambridge, Mass: Belknap Press of Harvard University Press, 1965), 266, hereafter cited in text as *Journals*.

4. Ralph Waldo Emerson, "Politics," in *The Early Lectures of Ralph Waldo Emerson*, vol. 3, ed. R. E. Spiller and W. E. Williams (Cambridge, Mass: Belknap Press of Harvard University Press, 1972), 240, hereafter cited in text as "Politics."

5. Tony Tanner, "Introduction" (*Europeans*, 22).

6. Nathaniel Hawthorne, *The Scarlet Letter and Selected Tales* (Harmondsworth: Penguin Books, 1970), 64, 66.

7. Nathaniel Hawthorne, *The Marble Faun* (New York: New American Library, 1961), vi.

8. Jean-Christophe Agnew, "The Consuming Vision of Her

in *The Culture of Consumption*, ed., R. W. Fox and T. J. Jackson Lears (New York: Pantheon Books, 1983), 84–85.

Chapter 13

1. This conflict was first noted in J. L. Winter, "The Chronology of *Washington Square*," *Notes and Queries*, N.S. 27, no.5 (October 1981): 426–28.

2. Quoted in Robert C. Le Clair, *Young Henry James: 1843–1870* (New York: Bookman Associates, 1955), 66.

3. Philip Fisher, *Hard Facts: Setting and Form in the American Novel* (New York and Oxford: Oxford University Press, 1985), 12–13.

BIBLIOGRAPHY

Primary Sources

Henry James

Edel, Leon, ed. *Henry James Letters*, 1875–1883, vol. 2. Cambridge, Mass: Belknap Press of Harvard University Press, 1975.

———. *Henry James Letters 1883–1895*, vol. 3. Cambridge, Mass. Belknap Press of Harvard University Press, 1980.

Edel, Leon, and Lyall H. Powers, eds. *The Complete Notebooks of Henry James.* New York and Oxford: Oxford University Press, 1987.

James, Henry. *The American*, edited by James W. Tuttleton. New York: W. W. Norton, 1978.

———. *The American Scene.* London: Macmillan, 1907.

———. *The Bostonians.* Harmondsworth: Penguin Books, 1966.

———. *Essays on Literature, American Writers, English Writers.* New York: Library of America, 1984.

———. *The Europeans.* Harmondsworth: Penguin Books, 1984.

———. *French Writers, Other European Writers, The Prefaces to the New York Edition.* New York: Library of America, 1984.

———. *Hawthorne*, edited by Tony Tanner. London: Macmillan, 1967.

———. *Washington Square.* Harmondsworth: Penguin Books, 1984.

Matthiessen, F. O., ed. *The American Novels and Stories of Henry James.* New York: Alfred A. Knopf, 1964.

Others

Johnson, Thomas H., ed. *The Complete Poems of Emily Dickinson* Little, Brown, 1960.

Emerson, Ralph Waldo. "Experience." In *Essays: Second Series*, 47–86. London: George Routledge and Sons, 1898.

———. *Nature*. In *The Collected Works of Ralph Waldo Emerson*, vol. 1, edited by R. E. Spiller and A. R. Ferguson, 7–45. Cambridge, Mass: Belknap Press of Harvard University Press, 1971.

———. "Politics." In *The Early Lectures of Ralph Waldo Emerson*, edited by R. E. Spiller and W. E. Williams, 238–47. Cambridge, Mass: Belknap Press of Harvard University Press, 1972.

Sealts, Merton, ed. *The Journals and Miscellaneous Notebooks of Ralph Waldo Emerson*, vol. 5. Cambridge, Mass: Belknap Press of Harvard University Press, 1965.

Hawthorne, Nathaniel. *The House of the Seven Gables*. In *The Centenary Edition of the Works of Nathaniel Hawthorne*, edited by William Charvat, Roy Harvey Pearce, and Claude M. Simpson. Columbus: Ohio State University Press, 1965.

———. *The Marble Faun*. In *Centenary Edition of the Works of Hawthorne*, 1968.

———. *The Scarlet Letter and Selected Tales*. Harmondsworth: Penguin Books, 1970.

Melville, Herman. *Billy Budd and Other Tales*. New York: New American Library, 1961.

Secondary Sources

Adorno, Theodor, and Max Horkheimer. *Dialectic of Enlightenment*, translated by John Cumming. London: New Left Books, 1979. Analysis of the commodification of culture.

Agnew, Jean-Christophe. "The Consuming Vision of Henry James." In *The Culture of Consumption*, edited by R. W. Fox and T. J. Jackson Lears, 67–100. New York: Pantheon Books, 1983. Reads James's later works as reflexes of an emergent consumer culture.

Babiiha, Thaddeo K. *The James-Hawthorne Relation*. Boston: G. K. Hall, 1980. Documents James's uses of Hawthorne's works.

———. "James's *Washington Square*: More on the Hawthorne Relation." *Nathaniel Hawthorne Journal* 4, no. 3 (Summer 1974): 270–72.

Roland. "Myth Today." In *Mythologies*, translated by Annette La- 109–59. St. Albans, Herts.: Paladin, 1973. Diagnoses the principal s of the bourgeois temperament.

Selected Bibliography

Bell, Ian F. A. "The Hard Currency of Words: Emerson's Fiscal Metaphor in *Nature.*" *English Literary History* 52, no. 3 (Fall 1985): 733–53.

Bell, Millicent, "Style as Subject: *Washington Square,*" *Sewanee Review* 83, no. 1 (Winter 1978): 19–38.

Bersani, Leo, "The Jamesian Lie," *Partisan Review* 36, no. 1 (Winter 1969): 53–79.

Bowlby, Rachel. *Just Looking: Consumer Culture in Dreiser, Gissing, and Zola.* London: Methuen, 1985. Study of consumerism's effects within fiction.

Buck, Norman Sidney. *The Development of the Organization of Anglo-American Trade 1800–1850.* Hamden, Conn: Archon Books, 1969. Economic history.

Buitenhuis, Peter. *The Grasping Imagination: The American Writings of Henry James.* Toronto: University of Toronto Press, 1970. Documents the American settings of James's works.

Conrad, Peter. *The Art of the City: Views and Versions of New York* Oxford and New York: Oxford University Press, 1984. Sections on James's uses of New York as fictional context.

Dietrichson, Jan W. *The Image of Money in the American Novel of the Gilded Age.* New York: Humanities Press, 1969. Sections on James's portrayals of wealth.

Dunne, Gerald T. *Justice Story and the Rise of the Supreme Court.* New York: Simon and Schuster, 1970. Legal history.

Dupee, F. W. *Henry James.* New York: William Sloane Associates, 1951. General survey of James's fiction.

Eagleton, Terry. *Criticism and Ideology.* London: New Left Books, 1976. Section on James and organic consciousness.

Edel, Leon. *The Life of Henry James.* 2 vols. Harmondsworth: Penguin Books, 1977. Standard biography of James.

Eliot, T. S. "The Hawthorne Aspect." In *The Shock of Recognition*, edited by Edmund Wilson, 858–65. London: W. H. Allen, 1956. Proposes the "native taste" of James through his relation to Hawthorne.

Feldberg, Michael. *The Turbulent Era: Riot and Disorder in Jacksonian America.* New York and Oxford: Oxford University Press, 1980. Social history.

Fisher, Philip. *Hard Facts: Setting and Form in the American Novel.* New York and Oxford: Oxford University Press, 1985. Examines the relations between art and social structures.

Freidel, Frank, and Norman Pollack, eds. *Builders of American Insti Readings in United States History.* Chicago: Rand-McNally, 1 lection of primary historical material from the seventeenth cer 1960s.

Gard, Roger, ed. *Henry James: The Critical Heritage*. London: Routledge and Kegan Paul, 1968. Collection of commentaries charting the history of the reception of James's works.

Geismar, Maxwell. *Henry James and the Jacobites*. Boston: Houghton Mifflin, 1963. General survey that seeks to reclaim James's achievement from the "cult of James" established since the 1940s.

Godden, Richard. "Some Slight Shifts in the Manner of the Novel of Manners." In *Henry James: Fiction as History*, edited by Ian F. A. Bell, 156–83. London and Totowa, N.J.: Vision Press and Barnes and Noble, 1984. Reads James through changes in the nature of the American economy.

Habegger, Alfred. *Henry James and the "Woman Business."* Cambridge: Cambridge University Press, 1989. Demonstrates the complexities and contradictions of James's presentations of the female.

———. *Gender, Fantasy, and Realism in American Literature*. New York: Columbia University Press, 1982. Chapters on James's preoccupations with gender in the context of literary realism.

Halttunen, Karen. *Confidence Men and Painted Women: A Study of Middle-Class Culture in America, 1830–1870*. New Haven: Yale University Press, 1982. Social history of style and manners.

Hammond, Bray. *Banks and Politics in America: From the Revolution to the Civil War*. Princeton, N.J.: Princeton University Press, 1957. Economic history.

Hofstadter, Richard. *The Paranoid Style in American Politics*. New York: Vintage Books, 1967. Essays on the structures of the American political imagination.

Hovey, Richard B. "*Washington Square*: James and 'The Deeper Psychology'," *Hartford Studies in Literature* 14, no. 1 (Fall 1982): 1–10.

Howells, William Dean. "James's *Hawthorne*." In *William Dean Howells as Critic*, edited by Edwin H. Cady, 50–55. London: Routledge and Kegan Paul, 1973. Review of James's monograph on Hawthorne.

Hutchinson, Stuart. *Henry James: An American as Modernist*. London: Vision Press, 1982. Finds James's modernity in his tendency to fabricate rather than imitate reality.

Kelley, Cornelia Pulsifer. *The Early Development of Henry James*, rev. ed. Urbana: University of Illinois Press, 1965. One of the earliest sustained accounts of James's technique.

ts, L. C., "Henry James and Human Liberty," *Sewanee Review* 83, no. Winter 1978): 1–18.

R. *The Great Tradition*. Harmondsworth: Penguin Books, 1967. rs on James locate him within a special line of English fiction.

Selected Bibliography

Le Clair, Robert C. *Young Henry James: 1843–1870*. New York: Bookman Associates, 1955. Biographical account of James's early years.

Lucas, John. "Washington Square." In *The Air of Reality: New Essays on Henry James*, edited by John Goode, 36–59. London: Methuen, 1972. Attends to the comic and disruptive effects of the novel.

Macdonald, William, ed. *Select Documents Illustrative of the History of the United States 1776–1861*. New York and London: Macmillan, 1898. Collection of primary historical material.

Maini, Darshan Singh, "*Washington Square*: A Centennial Essay," *Henry James Review* 1, no. 2 (Spring 1979): 81–101.

Martin, Jay. *Harvests of Change: American Literature 1865–1914*. Englewood Cliffs, N.J.: Prentice-Hall, 1967. Chapters on James read selected works in the context of the age.

Matthiessen, F. O. *Henry James: The Major Phase*. New York: Oxford University Press, 1963. General account of James's later works.

Meyers, Marvin. *The Jacksonian Persuasion*. Stanford, Calif.: Stanford University Press, 1957. Historical portrait of the 1830s and 1840s.

Miller, Douglas T. *Jacksonian Aristocracy: Class and Democracy in New York 1830–1860*. New York: Oxford University Press, 1967. Historical portrait of the 1830s and 1840s.

North, Douglass C. *The Economic Growth of the United States 1790–1860*. New York: W. W. Norton, 1966. Economic history.

Nugent, Walter T. K. *The Money Question during Reconstruction*. New York: W. W. Norton, 1967. Economic history.

Pessen, Edward. *Jacksonian America: Society, Personality, and Politics*, rev. ed. Homewood, Ill.: Dorsey Press, 1978. Historical portrait of the 1830s and 1840s.

Poirier, Richard. *The Comic Sense of Henry James*. London: Chatto and Windus, 1960. Study of James's early fiction.

Pound, Ezra. "Henry James." In *Literary Essays of Ezra Pound*, edited by T. S. Eliot, 295–338. London: Faber and Faber, 1960. Important early general survey of James's works.

Remini, Robert V. *Andrew Jackson and the Bank War*. New York: W. W. Norton, 1967. Economic history.

Richards, Leonard L. *"Gentlemen of Property and Standing": Anti-Abolition Mobs in Jacksonian America*. New York: Oxford University Press, 1970. Social and economic history.

Richardson, James F. *The New York Police: Colonial Times to 1901*. York: Oxford University Press, 1970. Chapter on social disorder the Jacksonian and Reconstruction periods.

Sharkey, Robert P. *Money, Class, and Party: An Economic Stu*

Civil War and Reconstruction. Baltimore, Md.: Johns Hopkins University Press, 1967. Economic history.

Sharp, James Roger. *The Jacksonians Versus the Banks*. New York: Columbia University Press, 1970. Economic history.

Shell, Marc, "The Gold Bug." *Genre* 13, no. 1 (Spring 1980): 11–30.

Sohn-Rethel, Alfred. *Intellectual and Manual Labour: A Critique of Epistemology*, translated by Martin Sohn-Rethel. London: Macmillan, 1978. Analysis of the bourgeois temperament.

Springer, Mary Doyle. *A Rhetoric of Literary Character: Some Women of Henry James*. Chicago: University of Chicago Press, 1978. Chapter on the role of Mrs. Penniman in *Washington Square*.

Stoehr, Taylor, "Words and Deeds in *The Princess Casamassima*," *English Literary History* 37, no. 1 (March 1970): 95–135.

Temin, Peter. *The Jacksonian Economy*. New York: W.W. Norton, 1969. Economic history.

Thomas, Brook. *Cross-Examinations of Law and Literature*. Cambridge: Cambridge University Press, 1987. Chapters on Hawthorne.

Unger, Irwin. *The Greenback Era: A Social and Political History of American Finance 1865–1879*. Princeton, N.J.: Princeton University Press, 1967. Economic history.

Veblen, Thorstein. *The Theory of the Leisure Class*. London: Unwin Books, 1970. Social and economic history of American institutions in the 1890s.

Volosinov, V. N. *Marxism and the Philosophy of Language*, translated by Ladislav Matejka and I. R. Titunik. New York: Seminar Press, 1973. A linguistic argument for the importance of dialogue in social relations.

West, Rebecca. *Henry James*. London: Nisbet and Co., 1916. The first sustained account of James's work.

INDEX

Index

Kenney, William, 104
Knights, L. C., 17, 84

Lawrence, D. H., 112
Leavis, F. R., 15
Leggett, William, 57
Lincoln, Abraham, 71
Locke, John, 39
Long, Robert Emmet, 16
Lucas, John, 13, 18, 96, 100, 104, 110–11

Maini, Darshan Singh, 19, 75, 89
Martin, Jay, 60
Matthiessen, F. O., 14, 15
Melville, Herman, 8, 19, 98–99, 100, 124
Miller, Douglas T., 43–44
Money, 5, 53, 68
Morgan, J. P., 145

Norris, Frank, 31
Nugent, Walter T. K., 61

Peabody, Elizabeth, 33
Pessen, Edward, 43
Poe, Edgar Allan, 55
Poirier, Richard, 17, 18, 110, 125
Pound, Ezra, 13–14, 40–41

Realism, 4, 10, 25, 28, 31, 36, 67

Romance, 4, 10, 26, 28, 31, 36, 67, 138
Ruskin, John, 145

Sainte-Beuve, Charles, 76
Schechter, Harold, 16
Shakespeare, William, 98–100
Sharp, James Roger, 56–57
Shell, Marc, 55–56, 69
Sohn-Rethel, Alfred, 51–52, 63–64, 68, 85, 102–103, 141
Springer, Mary Doyle, 15, 66–67, 104
Stevens, Wallace, 8
Stoehr, Taylor, 32, 62–63, 82, 83
Swedenborg, Emanuel, 71

Tanner, Tony, 25, 134
Taylor, John, 56
Thomas, Brook, 38–39, 68–69

Unger, Irwin, 61, 65

Veblen, Thorstein, 47
Volosinov, V. N., 81–82, 97–98, 102

Ward, J. A., 104
West, Rebecca, 13
Whitman, Walt, 8

Zola, Émile, 25, 37

THE AUTHOR

Ian F. A. Bell holds a Personal Chair in Literature in the Department of American Studies at the University of Keele. He received his B.A. in English and Philosophy from the University of Reading, where he also gained his Ph.D. for research into the works of Ezra Pound. He is the author of *Ezra Pound: Critic as Scientist, Henry James and the Past: Readings into Time*, and scholarly articles and essays on Pound, James, Emerson, Yeats, Eliot, and Cather, and editor of *Ezra Pound: Tactics for Reading, Henry James: Fiction as History*, and (with D. K. Adams) *American Literary Landscapes: The Fiction and the Fact*. He serves on the editorial boards of the *Journal of American Studies* and *Democratic Vistas*.